HISTORY of the

143RD REGIMENT

NEW YORK VOLUNTEERS, INFANTRY

SULLIVAN COUNTY

Editor: Robert G. Yorks

South Oxford Press
Oxford, NY 13830

Library of Congress Control Number: 2010915179

Published by
South Oxford Press
2139 County Road 3
Oxford, NY 13830
607-843-5629
southoxfordpress@live.com

Introduction

This is a transcription of the original document of the same title. We have kept most of the original spelling from that document, but in a few cases we have made corrections where they were needed.

We have not made any attempts to correct names of individuals, where they appear to be misspelled. Variations in the spelling of names was common in the 1700's and 1800's and we did not want to appear to be presumptuous in selecting one spelling over another.

In using the information in this book, be aware that the information in the 'Remarks' column, such as "Dead" was what was known on October 1, 1892. Generally that means that the individual died sometime between his discharge and Oct 1892.

We selected this particular regiment to transcribe because several of the volunteers in the regiment were ancestors of the editor.

We have added an every name index to the back of this publication to make it more convenient to locate specific individuals. We hope you find that to be useful.

Any corrections or comments can be directed to the editor using the information on the copyright page.

We sincerely hope that this publication will be welcomed and useful.

Respectfully submitted,

Robert G. Yorks

HISTORY of the
143RD REGIMENT
NEW YORK VOLUNTEERS, INFANTRY
SULLIVAN COUNTY

Recruited in August and September 1862
and Discharged July 20th, 1865

The 143d Regiment New York Infantry Volunteers was recruited in the counties of Sullivan and Tompkins. Companies A. B. C. E. F. G. H. & K. were recruited in Sullivan, D. & I. were first recruited in Tompkins but not being full were filled after coming to the 143d N. Y.

The first authority to recruit in Sullivan County, in 1862 was given by Col. Ellis, in July, he was then raising the 124th, which was to be raised in the counties of Orange and Sullivan; August 12th, 1862, authority was obtained to recruit a regiment in Sullivan and the companies forming for the 124th were turned over to the county organization. The regiment not filling up as fast as desired, arrangements were made with two companies then raising in Tompkins County. Capts. Higgins and Marvin brought what men they had, and some companies in Sullivan county, not filled, were consolidated with these two companies and some other of the companies not filled and the regiment was brought up to maximum strength.

The regiment went into camp at Camp
Holley, near Monticello, N.Y., early in
September, and companies D. and I. joined
the regiment the last of September. The
regiment was mustered in by Lieut. Crowley,
for 3 years, Oct. 8th, 1862, and the
regimental colors were presented by the
citizens of Sullivan county, October 9th.
Hon. O. B. Wheeler made the presentation
speech. The regiment started for the front,
October 10th, 1862, marched to Middletown,
N. Y., from there by rail; they lay some two
days in New York city, in barracks then
standing where the present Post Office
building is situated.

When they reached Washington they were
assigned to the defenses of that city, and
put on picket and fatigue duty in Virginia,
and were camped at Upton's Hill, Va., first,
then later at near Cloud's Mills,Va, and in
April, 1863, they were sent with other
troops to the relief of Suffolk, Va. After
the siege of Suffolk, was raised, with other
troops, under Gen. Keys, went to West Point,
Va., and after Chancellorsville was fought
they went to Yorktown, Va., June 1st, and
then up to White House, Va., reaching there
June 27th and starting back for Yorktown
July 8th, reaching there 10th inst. and so
on to the transports, and sent to
Washington, and from there by rail, to Fred-
erick City, Md., which place was reached
July 12, and then was sent out to reinforce
Meade's Army, then lying near Hunkstown, Md.
A few days later Gen. Meade's army followed
Lee's army into Virginia and the regiment
crossed the Potomac, near Berlin, Va., and

marched to near Warrington Junction, Va.,
where they went into camp. They lay until
in September, 1863, when, after the battle
of Chickamauga, Ga., was fought by Gen.
Rosecrans, Gen. Joseph Hooker was sent west
to the relief of Gen. Rosecrans at
Chattanooga, Tenn, with the 11th and 12th
Army Corps.

They went by rail to Bridgeport, Ala.,
and there these two corps began a campaign
that, after fighting the battle of
Wauhatchie, Tenn, Oct 29th, 1863, resulting
in opening the cracker road to Chattanooga,
the regiment with the 11th and 12th corps
was in Lookout Valley, Tenn., until the
battle of Missionary Ridge, and the day
before that battle began, the division, in
which the regiment belonged, was put just
night into the company streets of the 14th
corps and the first day was among troops
that moved against the enemy's center at
Orchard Knob. The 2nd day's fighting they
were among the troops sent by Gen. Grant to
the left to A and were at the last of the
battle on left of the army and as soon as
Braggs army was routed the regiment, with
other troops, under Gens. Sherman and
Howard, were sent to the relief of Gen.
Burnsides force, at Knoxville, Tenn.

The whole command were in light
marching order, having left knapsacks, etc,
in camp, and were stripped for battle before
going into Missionary Ridge. It was cold
weather,rained and snowed part of the time
and froze hard, and the troops suffered
severely from the cold and insufficient

protection from the storms. The only way
they could keep from perishing, at night,
was by burning large fires, (sometimes in
parallel lines and lying between the fires,
feet towards the fire and heads in the
center) and sleeping beside them. At Louden,
Tenn., Dec. 4th and 5th, 1863, the regiment
was detailed to bridge the Little Tennessee
river, a wide swift river some 300 yards
wide, which they bridged between 7 pm and 5
am, making most of the bridge of wagons with
two planks from bolster and from wagon to
wagon. The last of benches, where the
water was deepest, and many of the men were,
of necessity, in the cold water, and it was
so cold a man coming out of the water he
could not get to the top of the river bank
before his clothes were frozen stiff.

After relieving Gen. Burnside the
troops marched and went into camp at Lookout
Valley, for a short time, and in January
1864, moved to Bridgeport, Ala., and went
into winter quarters, where they lay until
the Atlanta campaign opened. The 11th and
12th corps were consolidated and formed the
20th corps and Gen. Hooker in command. The
Atlanta campaign opened in May, 1864, the
battle of Rockey Faced Gap, Ga. opened the
campaign but the battle of Resaca,Ga., May
13th, 14th and 15th, 1864, was the first
pitched battle of the campaign. After Resaca
and Johnston fell back, the 143rd bridged
one of the branches of the Etowah RIver in a
short time so the infantry crossed on it.

From May 25th, 1864, when the battle of Pumpkinvine Creek, Ga., opened, to July 3rd, 1864 it was about one continuous fighting and skirmishing and during which the enemy's positions of Altoona and Kenesaw Mountains were completely turned and fell into our army's hands. After maneuvering, our army succeeded in getting on the south side of the Chattahoucha river and July 20 the battle of Peach Tree Creek, Ga., was fought. The investment of the city of Atlanta, by works, began July 22d, building heavy works, and from the last date to latter part of August the regiment was in exposed position in the line of investment, and almost constantly some portion, if not all of it, was under fire.

The 20th corps occupied the city of Atlanta, Sep. 2nd, 1864, and during the Atlanta campaign from May 7, 1864, to latter part of August, 1864, some portion of the regiment were almost daily under fire and men of the regiment, wounded early in that campaign, rejoined their command before it was over. They lay at Atlanta, Ga., until Nov. 15, 1864, when Gen. Sherman moved out and began his campaign against Savannah, Ga., passing through Milledgeville, Ga., and several smaller towns.

Gen. Sherman's army invested the city of Savannah, Dec. 10th, 1864, and the 143d was represented on the skirmish and picket line that day. The city surrendered, Dec. 22nd, 1864, and on or about January 15th or 16th, 1865, Sherman began his campaign through the Carolinas. Near Robertsville, S. C., the first brush with the enemy was had, 143d N.Y. skirmishing. They fell back and Sherman's troops occupied the town. This campaign opened with swollen streams and mud and they had to march often from knee to waist deep in water, and were at Fayette-ville, N. C., early in March, where the army rested a day or two. The day after it moved on, the battle of Averysboro, N. C., was fought, (March 16th, 1865) and three days later, March 19th, the battle of Benton-ville, N.C. began. The brigade to which the regiment belonged, occupied the ground Carlin's Division of the 14th corps were forced to fall back from. The 143d was on the extreme left, with no connections on their left flank, but held their ground for several hours and until night set in. The commander of the division, after that fight, said the 143d, N. Y., was made of staying qualities.

Sherman's army occupied Goldsboro, N.C., March 25th, 1865. His troops lay there until after Lee's surrender when he marched to intercept General Johnston's army, and after some fighting resulted in the surrender of Johnston's army, then the whole of Gen. Sherman's army marched to Washington, D. C., were reviewed May 24th, 1865, and was disbanded, and the regiment was put into a temporary brigade and lay near Washington until July 20th, 1865, when it was mustered out of service and sent to New York city to be paid off and disbanded.

The regiment was reviewed at New York City by General Joseph Hooker and city officials, and General Hooker in front of the Astor House said a few words to the boys. He told them he was not given to speech making, but that he could not let the regiment disband without saying a word to them. After thanking them for the many times they had stood to their places he said "it could be said of them what could not be said of many regiments, he did not know as of any others -- the Johnnys had never seen their backs: that if they had at Peach Tree Creek, God only knows what the result would have been."

The 143d New York were in the
4d Brigade, Abercrombie's Division from October 16, 1862,
in the 22d Corps from February 1863;
in 3d Hughston's Brigade, Gurney's Division Department, Virginia, at Suffolk, Virginia, from April 1863;
in 1st Brigade Gordon's of 7th Corps, from May 1863;
in the 4th Corps from June, 1863;
in 1st Brigade, 3d Division, 11 Corps, from July 14, 1863;
in 3d Brigade, 1st Division, 20th Corps, from April, 1864;
in 2d Brigade, Bartlett's Division, 22d Corps from June 30, 1865

The 143d New York took part in:
-The siege of Suffolk, Virginia, April and
    May, 1863
-Battle of Nansemond, Virginia, May 3d, 1863
-Under General Keys on Peninsula, Virginia,
    May, June and July, 1863;
-Battle of Wauhatchie, Tennessee, October
    28 and 29, 1863;
-Battle of Missionary Ridge and vicinity,
    November 23, 24 and 25, 1863;
-The relief of Knoxville, Tennessee,
    November and December, 1863;
-The Atlanta Campaign, May 2d to September
    2d, 1864;
-Battle of Resaca, Georgia, May 13, 14 and
    15, 1864;
-Battle of Cassville, Georgia, May 19th to
    22d, 1864
-Battle of Pumpkinvine Creek, Georgia, May
    25, 1864;
-Battles around Ackworth, Kenesaw Mountain,
    Lost Mountain, Big Shanty, Marietta,
    Golgotha, Nose Creek and Culps Farm,
    June 4 to July 2, 1864;
-Battle of Peach Tree Creek, July 20, 1864;
-Siege of Atlanta, July 22 to August 26,
    1864;
-Atlanta to Savannah, "March to the Sea,"
    November 15 to December 22, 1864;
-Battle of Montieth Swamp, Georgia,
    December 9, 1864;
-Campaign of the Carolinas, January 17 to
    April 26, 1865;
-Battle of Robertsville, S.C., Jan. 29 1865;
-Battle of Lawtonville, S.C., Feb 2, 1865;
-Battle of Averysboro, N.C., March 16,
    1865;
-Battle of Bentonville, N.C., March 19,
    1865;

-Battle near Goldsboro, N.C., March 27, 1865;
-Battle near Akin Creek, N.C., April 10, 1865;
-Battle near Bennett House, N.C., April 26, 1865.

GENERAL HORACE BOUGHTON,

appointed to the Colonelcy of the 143d Regiment after the resignation of Colonel Dewitt, was born at Rust, New York, March 23d, 1833, and was educated at the Genesee Weslyean Seminary and Genesee College. He studied law at Rochester, where in April 1861 he enlisted and was made First Lieutenant in the Thirteenth New York Volunteer Infantry. Later he was made Captain of his company. In the fall of 1862 he was commissioned Lieutenant Colonel of the 143d Regiment and 1865 he was made Brigadier General of Volunteers for "faithful and meritorious services." From 1866 to 1870 he was United States Revenue Collector for the 4th District of Texas. For nearly twenty years General Boughton was an invalid, having sustained partial paralysis, the result of exposure while in active service. He died at Washington November 8th, 1891.

GENERAL DAVID PORTER DeWITT

the first Colonel of the 143d Regiment, was
born in Hoboken, N. J., July 10th, 1817, and
in June, 1832, entered the West Point
Military Academy from which he graduated in
June 1836. On his graduation he was
commissioned as Second Lieutenant in the
United States Second Artillery. He resigned
his commission in the army to accept a
position as engineer in the survey and
location of the Erie Railroad which was then
being built. He continued in the employ of
the Erie company until 1857, when he went to
Canada and located the Ontario, Simcoe and
Huron Railroad. In 1859 he entered the
service of the United States Express
Company; in 1861 on the breaking out of the
war, he was commissioned Major of the Mary-

land Volunteers. In March 1862 he was
commissioned Colonel of the 3d Maryland
Regiment, and served in Virginia under
General Banks and General Pope,
participating in the battles of Cedar
Mountain and Beverly Ford. Active service
reduced the 3d Maryland to 250 men, and he
resigned its command and was commissioned
Colonel of the 143d Regiment. In July 1863,
on account of disease contracted in the
service, he resigned from the 143d, and was
made Major in the 10th Veteran Reserve
Corps, of which he was made Colonel in
August 1863. In 1865 he was made Brigadier
General for "faithful and meritorious
services." Death closed his distinguished
and useful career at Middletown, Orange
County, NY, on Tuesday, February 26th, 1889.

Field and Staff 143d Regiment New York Infantry Volunteers

NAME	RANK	REMARKS	LAST KNOWN P.O. ADDRESS
Horace Boughton	Col., Died Nov.1891 and Brevet Gen. USA		Washington, D.C.
Hezekiah Watkins	Lieut. Col and Brevet Col. U.S.A.	Died Feb 12, 1884	
Rensselaer Hammond	Adjutant		Lansing, Kan.
David Matthews	Surgeon	Died at NY City July 10, 1891	
Wm. H. Stuart	Asst. Surgeon		Norwich, NY
Edward C. Howard	Quar.	Dead	
David P. DeWitt	Colonel	Discharged Apr 29, 1863, died at Middletown, NY	
John Higgins	Major	Discharged May 16 1865, for wounds & died at Ithaca, NY January 15, 1888.	
Wallace W. Wheeler	Quar.	Discharged Dishonorably, March 26, 64	
Henry M. Edsall	Surgeon	Discharged Feb. 28, 1863, died at Wurtsboro, NY	
Orrin A. Carroll	Surgeon	Discharged Oct. 8th, 1863 died at Port Jervis, NY	
Herman Craft	Asst. Surgn.	Disch'd April 11, '64. Stone Ridge, NY	
Jeremiah Searle	Chaplain	Discharged Mch. 2, '63	
Isaac Gilbert	Chaplain	" Aug. 29, '63	
Edgar K. Apgar	Adjutant	Feb 1, '63 discharged, died at Albany, NY	
Joseph B. Taft	Lt. Colonel	Killed in action, Nov 25, 1863 Missionary Ridge, GA	
Wm. B. Ratcliff	Adjutant	Killed in action, July 20, 1864 at Peach Tree Creek, GA	

Non-Commissioned Staff

NAME	RANK	REMARKS	LAST KNOWN P.O. ADDRESS
Jas. A. Eickenbergh	Sgt Major		Warren, PA
Seneca W. Perry	Quar. Sergt.	Dead	
Jon C. Hardenburgh	Hospital Stewt		Phillipsport, NY
August Rambour	Principal Musician		Monticello, NY
Chas. J. McPherson	" "		New York City

ABSENT, NOT MUSTERED OUT WITH REGIMENT

George Sturdevant   Commissary Sergt   Bethel, NY

DISCHARGED

DeWitt Apgar   Sergt Major Dec 31 1863, for promotion.
Char. W. J. Hardenburgh   "   "   Sept 6, '64 for promotion.
                                        Died from wound battle of
                                        Averysboro, NC
William T. Morgan   Sergt Major April 25 1865 for promotion
                                        Died at Middletown

TRANSFERRED

Abram Laraway   Quar. Sergt Reduced to ranks Jan 16 '64
                                        tramped to Co. A.   Dead.
John A. Foster   "   "   Reduced to ranks Nov 22 '64
                                        tramped to Co. K.   Dead.

Co. "A" 143d N.Y.V. Infantry
Mustered out with the Company July 20th, 1865.
Special Order No. 160, Headquarters Washington
Discharge Given

NAME	RANK	REMARKS	LAST KNOWN P.O. ADDRESS
William T. George	Captain		Kirkville, Mo.
Joseph Pierce	1st Lieut.		
David A. Wasim	2d "		Died at Liberty, NY
Samuel Lord	1st Sergt.		Parksville, NY
Thomas H. Litts	Sergeant		Monticello, NY
George R. Wright	"		
William H. Myers	"		Gilman's Depot, NY
William D. Myers	"		Died July 21, 1891
Wilson Laraway	Corporal		Livingston Manor, NY
Herman M. Krum	"		Liberty, NY
George H. Akins	"		Livingston Manor, NY
Moses Young	"		Brooklyn, NY
William H. Ashton	"		Fremont, NY
Thomas Bates	"		Brooklyn, NY
Martimus Laraway	Wagoner		Gilboa, NY
Allen, Archibald C.	Private		Monticello, NY
Baily, Charles A.	"		
Brown, James L.	"		
Baker, David B.	"		
Brown, Albert	"		
Cammer, Joseph	"		Rockland, NY
Cantrell, John	"		Toledo, Ohio
Cantrell, Thomas	"		
Casterline, Edward	"		
Conor, Thomas A.	"		
Corgal, Thomas	"		
Cox, Abraham	"		Fremont Cntr, NY
Corby, Orrin B.	"		White Lake, NY
Eldridge, George D.	"		Mongaup Valley, NY
Gregory, Stephen J.	"		Stevensville, NY
Hollis, Charles S.	"		Carbondale, PA
Housten, Edmund	"		Winchester, VA
Hunt, John	"		
Haight, Walter T.	"		
Josclyn, John W.	"		Shin Creek, NY
Keeler, Bailey S.	"		Middletown, NY
Keeler, David H.	"		Middletown, NY
Laraway, Henry	"	Dead	
Laraway, Abrm.	"	Dead	
Lord, James	"		
Miller, Samuel J.	"		Died at Bethel, NY
Morris, George J.	"		Liberty, NY
Myers, Moses D., Jr.	"		
Newman, Thomas	"		

Osborn, Peter V.	Private	Haverstraw, NY
Purvis, George W.	"	Binghamton, NY
Richard, Louis P.	"	
Robertson, Levi	"	Ashgrove, Neb.
Smith, Arthur W.	"	
Stratton, George W.	"	Adison, NY
Taggett, Henry F.	"	Haworth, NJ
Thompson, John	"	
Walee, John	"	Died at Liberty, NY
York(s), Herman	"	[Died at Kingsley, MI] Ed. note
Quackenbush, Franklin	"	

Absent, Not mustered out with company

Beebe, Roswell T.	Corporal	Minneapolis, MN
Allen, Seymour R.	Private	
Black, John	"	
Coleman, Henry B.	"	Murfreysboro, TN
Darling, David	"	
Decker, William N.	"	
Fisher, William J.	"	
Fisher, Peter A.	"	Scranton, PA
Foot, Edward F.	"	Wurtsboro, NY
Keen, Gilbert	"	Died at Rockland NY
Kanise, Louis	"	North Branch, NY
McMillen, William	"	New York City
Smith, George	"	In Kansas
Terry, Seth A.	"	Washington, DC
Travis, George W.	"	
Wright, Charles	"	
Wood, Hezekiah	"	

Discharged

Hezekiah Watkins	Captain, Jan. 1, 1864 promoted to Major. Died at Middletown, NY
George Young	2d Lieut., Jan. 1, 1864 promoted to 1st Lieutenant and wounded July 20, 1864. Discharged Oct. 26, 1864 Ellenville, NY
Dewitt Apgar	2d Lieut., Promoted 1st Lieut. NY City
George C. Penney	2d Lieut., Promoted 1st Lieut. Damascus, PA
Wallace Hill	1st Sergt., Promoted 1st Lieutenant Scranton, PA
Charles A. Smith	1st Sergt., Promoted 1st Lieutenant Monticelle, NY
Philo Buckley	1st Sergt.,
Allen, John M.	Private Dover, TN
Allen, William C.	" Monticello, NY
Burns, Frederick W.	" Oakland Valley, NY
Cantrell, Edward R.	" For disability
Drennon, Robert	"
Dice, Henry	"
Everard, Eleasor	" Scranton, PA
Gregory, Stephen P.	" March 4, 1863
Hoxie, William W.	" June 19, 1865

Hadden, James H.	Priv.	General Order 77
Hodge, James H.	"	Telegram Order
Lohman, Adam	"	June 11, 1865
Lent, Nath'l V.	"	Telegram Order
McCord, Andrew J.	"	Jan. 13, 1864
Middaugh, Denis S.	"	April 17, 1864, Dead
Myers, Adelbert	"	General Order 77
Mason, James B.	"	General Order 77
Sheely, David J.	"	General Order 77 Pine Bush, NY
Sheeley, Tobias	"	General Order 77
Smith, William	"	General Order 77, Died
Wagner, Frank	"	Dec. 19, 1863, Dead
Whiston, David W.	"	May 29, 1865

TRANSFERRED

Bennett, William	Priv.	To Vet. Res. Corps
		Livingston Manor, NY
Hoyt, Lewis N.	"	" Nineva, NY
Hunt, Abrm.C.	"	" Stevensville, NY
Oudet, C.G.A	"	" Dead.
Rambour, August	"	To Com's Staff Monticello, NY
Sturdevant, George	"	" Bethel, NY
Smith, Orrin B.	"	To Vet. Res. Corps, Staff
		Monticello, NY
McPherson, Charles J.	"	Non Coms. Staff, New York City

DIED

Alberly, Thomas	Priv.	Jan. 13, 1863, Uptons Hill, VA
Beebe, Joseph L.	"	Oct. 5, 1864, Chattooga, TN
		from wounds at Peach Tree
		Creek, GA
Carpenter, John W.	"	July 17, 1863, Portsmouth, VA
Dobbs, Michael	"	July 19, 1863, Chespeak Hosp.
Dodge, Cyrus	"	Feb. 2, 1864, Murfresboro, TN
Everdon, Edwin, J.	"	Killed July 20, 1864, Peach
		Tree Creek
Lord, Joseph H.	"	Nov. 7, 1864 near Alexander, VA
Lounsbury, John M.	"	Nov. 12, 1864 of wound July 20,
		at Peach Tree Creek, Ga.
Mapledoram, James C.	"	Dec 20, 1863 Lookout Valley, TN
McWilliams, John	"	July 21, 1864 Peach Tree Cr, GA
Mead, William H.	"	Dec 11, 1863 Athens, GA
Price, James	"	Dec 24, 1864 Savannah, GA
Tillotson, Robert L.	"	Jan 15, 1864 Yorktown, VA
VanOrden, Peter	"	July 22, 1864, wounded at Peach
		Tree Ridge, GA
VanSiclen, Theodore C.	"	Killed July 26, 1864 Peach Tree
		Creek, GA
Young, Gilbert I.	"	Aug 5, 1864 wounded at Peach
		Tree Creek, Kingston, GA
Amos P. Akins	Sgt	Killed July 20, 1864 Peach Tree
		Creek, GA
John E. Purvis	Corp.	Jan 18, 1863 Yorktown, VA

Co. "B" 143d N.Y.V. Infantry

Mustered out with the Company July 20th, 1865.
Special Order No. 160, Headquarters Washington
Discharge Given

NAME	RANK	REMARKS	LAST KNOWN P.O. ADDRESS
Isaac Jelliff	1st Lieut.		Woodbourne, NY
William Smith	1st Sgt		Bethel, NY
Renwick Brown	Sergeant		Cheboygan, MI
Robert Cantrell	"		Monticello, NY
Lewis S. Wheeler	"		Liberty Falls, NY
Philip S. Robison	Corporal		
Summer H. Dunn	"		Trout Brook, NY
Uriah M. Brodhead	"		Fremont Ctr, NY
Christopher Bolhman	"		Binghamton, NY
Lorenzo Secor	"		
Benjamin F. Allyn	Musician		Monticello, NY
Black, John	Private		Centreville, NY
Conklin, Eugene	"		
Cromwell, Alexander	"		
Decker, Chas. H. D.	"		Oakland Valley NY
Earnest, Adam	"		
Foot, Shubal	"	Dead	
Kent, Jacob	"		Stevensville, NY
Kent, Rurr S.	"		
Loring, Jonathan C.	"		Monticello, NY
Morris, James D.	"		
Rumsey, Cyrus	"		Thompsonville, NY
Rumsey, John J.	"		Fostara, Ohio
Ralston, George	"		
Smith, James	"		Rolfe, PA
Waddell, Niel H.	"		
Wright, Joseph	"		White Lake, NY
Watts, John C.	"		
Watts, George B.	"		
Yeomans, William H.	"		Hartwood, NY
McIntyre, John L.	"		Robinssonville NY
Joyner, Joseph	"		

ABSENT, NOT MUSTERED OUT WITH COMPANY

Benjamin Bates	Sergeant		Sparrowbush, NY
Isaac C. France	Corporal		Fairfax, VA
Crosby, Scipio L.	"		Cochecton Ctr, NY
Ferguson, James	"		
Geary, Dan	"		
Kent, George A.	"		
Lybolt, Henry C.	"		Monticello, NY
Palmer, Asha B.	"	Dead	
Slater, Albert H.	"		Eureka, NY

Stanton, Charles C.   Corporal   Bethel, NY
Weber, Sohn   "

DISCHARGED

Alfred J. Baldwin   Captain Dismissed the service by
                                  General Order May 6, 1864. Died
                                  at Monticello, NY
Lyan, S. Linson   Sergeant Died at Stevensville, NY, May
                                  4, 1864, promoted.
David A. Wasim   1st Sgt June 19, 1865, promoted, Dead
Richard J. Hardenburgh Sgt. April 17, 1863, promoted Ser-
                                  geant Major. Killed in Action.
Dan M. Freeman   Corp.   Jan. 28, 1863
John H. Jacobs   Corp.   June 16, 1865
Will. D. Sisson   Corp.   June 29, 1863
Bowman Melchoir   Priv.   Aug 31, 1863   Monticello, NY
Cantine, Nicholas S.   "   See order   Middletown, NY
Clark, Garrett T.   "   May 28, 1865 P. Rolfe, PA
Durland, James   "   June 30, 1865. Dead
Jackson, Dan   "   Nov 14 1863.   Dead
Lorgan, James D.   "   Dec 12, 1863
Perry, Seneca W.   "   Nov 22, 1864. Dead
Rose, Austin J.   "   Dec 24, 1863   Thompsonville, NY
Tucker, William   "   March 23, 1864
Haines, George N.   "   By General Order
Palmer, Rufus   "   "
Travis, Orrin   "   "
Vantran, John   "   "   Woodbourne, NY

TRANSFERRED

Edward C. Howard   1st Lieut., promoted to Quartermaster,
                                  Dead
Leander T. Brown   Sgt.   Aug 1, 1863, Signal Corps, NYC
Patterson, John   Corp.   July 1, 1863   Monticello, NY
Avery, William L.   Priv.   May 1, 1864.   Dead
Putler, Patrick   "   Nov 15, 1863. Dead
Cumfort, Rieve   "   April 30, 1864 Montgomery, NY
Fisher, Ira   "   July 1, 1863. Dead
Stanton, John S.   "   Nov 15, 1863
Warring, Hiram B.   "   July 1, 1863

DIED

Edward Carrington   2d Lieut. Killed in action
Abrm. S. Fredmore   Sgt   Jan 29, 1863 conveles-
                                  cent camp.
John C. Pentlar   "   Jan 29, Nashville, TN
Gustavus, Rose   Corp.   Aug 1, 1864, Lookout Mt., TN
John H. Jackson   "   Mar 28, 1863 Alexander, VA
Bloemingburgh, Wm. J.   Priv.   Mar 20, Alexander, VA
Brown, Marcus L.   "   July 16, 1863, Fort Monroe, VA

Bollman, Christopher S.	Priv.	Sept 30, 1863, Indianapolis, IN
Brown, Orvil A.	"	Apr 2, 1864, Murfresboro, TN
Carpenter, Will. L.	"	Mar 30, 1863, Alexandria, VA
Carpenter, Benjamin	"	Jan 30, 1864, Indianapolis, IN
Cogswell, Richard	"	Mar 7, 1864, Louisville, KY
Demerest, Jonathan O.	"	Mar 20, 1863, Alexandria, VA
Durland, Stephen D.	"	Oct 31, 1864, near Dallas, GA
Frasier, Will. J.	"	Nov 21, 1863, Nashville, TN
Fitzgerald, James	Priv.	Dec 12, 1863, Athens, TN
Hogancamp, John M.	"	Mar 20, 1863, Alexandria, VA
Hendrickson, John M.	"	
Hosa, John	"	
Krum, Luther S.	"	Mar 1863, Killed R.R. Alexandria, VA
Kent, Charles	"	
Kinne, Dan L.	"	Killed at Bentonville, NC
Lyon, George	"	
Lawson, Benjamin	"	
Oneil, Terrace	"	
Pentlar, Will.	"	
Ray, Edward	"	
Sutter, Henry	"	
Warring, John W.	"	
Whitley, George W.	"	
White, Joe	"	
Watson, Martin	"	Died at Uptons Hill, VA
Yorks, Nicholas	"	
Yeomans, Benj. M.	"	

DESERTED

David H. Wagner	Corp.	Dec. 16, 1862, Washington

Co. "C" 143d N.Y.V. Infantry

Mustered out with the Company July 20th, 1865.
Special Order No. 160, Headquarters Washington
Discharge Given

NAME	RANK	REMARKS	LAST KNOWN P.O. ADDRESS
William R. Bennett	Capt.		Hutchinson, KS
Henry H. Hemingway	1st Lieut.		Petersburgh, VA
Bruce Elmore	"	Dead.	
George V. Manett	Sergeant		New Tacoma, W.T.
Henry Eberlin	"		Roscoe, NY
McKendru N. Dodge	"		Rockland, NY
John W. Darbee	"		Rockland, NY
James C. DeKay	Corporal		Rutland, VT
Abner J. Coddington	"		Divines Corners, NY
Charles Wicks	"	Died in PA	
William H. Newman	"	Dead	
James W. Stewart	"		Hurleyville, NY
Willard Elmore	"		S. Fallsburgh, NY
James Low	Musician		
Bowers, Alfred	Private		Kingsley, MI
Brown, William B.	"		Meredith Hollow, NY
Briggs, William A.	"		Claryville, NY
Brown, Albert N.	"		Hasbrouck, NY
Coddington, Monroe	"		Hurleyvill, NY
Cauthers, Henry A.	"		Centerville Stat, NY
Conklin, Benjamin	"	Dead:1888	
Cross, Cornelius	Private		
Denniston, John G.	"		Fallsburgh, NY
Doloway, Stephen L.	"		Boyd's Mills, PA
Furch, George	"		
Fincle, William	"		East Port, MD
Gorton, John T.	"		Neversink, NY
Gorton, James D.	"		Grahamsville, NY
Gardener, Austin	"		S. Fallsburgh, NY
Hornbeck, John	"		
Lawrence, Peter E.	"		Divines Corners, NY
Leslie, James E.	"		Brooklyn, NY
Lewis, Reuben A.	"		
Lewis, William B.	"		Debruce, NY
Morgan, Isaac	"		St. Louis, MI
Maricle, William P.	"	Dead.	
Palmer, John J.	"	Dead.	
Shultis, Wm. H.	"	Dead.	
Tripp, Peter C.	"		Kane, PA
Upham, George W.	"		Hasbrouck, NY
Vredenburgh, Jacob C.	"	Dead.	
Van Wagner, George W.	"		Livingston Manor, NY

ABSENT NOT MUSTERED OUT WITH COMPANY

Samuel A. Row	Corporal	
Barnhart, Wm.	Private	Montgomery, NY
Cross, George W.	"	He was seriously wounded at Pumpkin Vine Creek, GA, May 25, 1865, and sent to Gen. Hosp., and Lieut. Palen, commanding that day, believes he died at hospital.
Everett, George H.	"	Neversink, NY
Hitt, Franklin	"	Port Jervis, NY
Whittaker, Henry	"	S. Fallsburgh, NY

DISCHARGED

James C. French	Capt. March 6, 1863, resigned
Nathaniel C. Clark	1ˢᵗ Lieut., Feb 8, 1864, Special Order
John R. Groo	" Jan 10, '64. special order, NYC
Dwight Divine	2d Lieut., For promotion April 1, '64
Peter E. Palen	1ˢᵗ Lieut., For promotion May 1, 1864
James B. Wilson	Sergeant, Oct 11, 1864, disability. Sacramento, CA
Adna L. Knox	Corp., Feb 17, 1864 Port Jervis, NY
George Atwell	" June 24, 1865, Gen. Order, Dead
William Hill	" Feb 27, 1865, disability.
Bowers, Palmer	Priv. Dec 18, 1862
Cox, Joseph E.	" Dec 26, 1863, disability.
Conklin, Theodore	" April 14, 1863, Debruce, NY
Dennis, William	" Feb 23, 1864
Finch, Isaac N.	" Feb 9, 1863 Stone Ridge, NY
Hendrixson, Wm	" Feb 13, 1864, died at Woodbourne, NY
Lockwood, Daniel C.	" April 27, 1863
Low, Jonathan W.	" May 3, 1865, Dead.
Meddeuch, Abrm	" Never mustered in act of injury received.
Meddler, Wm. O.	Priv., April 23, 1863, Peakville, NY
Perhamous, Emery	" Jan 19, 1863 Walker Valley, NY
Patmore, David A.	" May 16, 1865 Ridgeway, PA
Reynolds, Nelson T.	" Mar 20, 1863 Hurleyville, NY
Sprague, DeWitt C.	" June 17, 1865 Parksville, NY
Starr, Sanford M.	" Mar 5, 1863 Monticello, NY
Tyrell, William	" June 9, 1865 Mount Hope, NY
Taylor, William J.	" Dec 10, 1862, Dead.
Vredenburgh, Henry J.	" June 1, 1863, Dead.
Vredenburgh, Henry H.	" Aug 18, 1863,Livingston Manor NY
Wilson, Andrew S.	" Apr 13, 1863 Centreville, NY
Bennett, Asa A.	" General Order Rosco, NY
Bennett, Miller P.	" " Rosco, NY
Chapman, Jones	" " Rockland, NY
Darbee, Cleveland	" " Rosco, NY
Darbee, John A.	" " Liberty, NY

Demunn, Francis M.	Priv.	"	Gage Gates Co. NY
Hood, George W.	"	"	Tug River, WV
Matthews, Lorenzo	"	"	Livingston Manor, NY
Martin, Gideon W.	"	"	
Powell, Russell	"	"	
Rowe, Orrin D.	"	"	Lew Beach, NY
Swarthout, Alex. E.	"	"	Hurleyville, NY
Stratton, Cyrus J.	"	"	Thompsonville, NY
Terwilliger, Benj.	"	By Telegram	Divines Crns, NY

TRANSFERRED

Tobias C. Sheeley	Sgt	Dec 1, 1863	Newburgh, NY
Ferdon, Anthony C	Priv	To Company F.	Rosco, NY
Jones, Benj.	"	July 1, 1863	Fallsburgh, NY
Miller, David	"	July 1, 1863	Centerville, NY
Newman, Austin D.	"	May 15, 1864	Fallsburgh, NY
Schoonmaker, Moses	"	May 15, 1863	Thompsonville, NY
Wamsley, John	"	Sept 30, 1863	Shin Creek, NY

DIED

James M. Hitt	Sgt.	April 11, 1863
Jonathan Jones	"	Dec 5, 1863
Barnhart, Herman	Priv.	Oct 29, 1863
Barkley, Anthony	"	Oct 7, 1863
Black, James A.	"	Nov 5, 1863
Donaldson, John B.	"	Feb 5, 1864
Hendrickson, Blake	"	June 30, 1863
Hill, Matthew	"	Dec 2, 1864
Lawrence, Gilbert	"	July 26, 1864 of wounds rec'd.
Mackney, Samuel	"	June 1, 1864, drowning accident
Maltby, Marcus	"	May 20, 1863
Perkey, Elijah P.	"	Apr 15, 1864
Roosa, John E.	"	Oct 8, 1863
Roosa, Francis M.	"	Oct 21, 1864
Simpson, Chas. H.	"	Nov 26, 1863
Schoonmaker, Moses H.	"	July 26, 1863
Terwilliger, Sevryn M.	"	Nov 6, 1863
Taylor, James M.	"	Jan 31, 1864
White, Abrm.	"	July 20, 1863

DESERTED

Bowers, Herman	Priv.	April 30, 1863
Dewitt, John	"	July 14, 1863
Gorton, Nelson	"	July 14, 1863 Pardoned and dis-charged May 30, 1865
Leroy, Peter H.	"	April 30, 1863

Co. "D" 143d N.Y.V. Infantry
Mustered out with the Company July 20th, 1865.
Special Order No. 160, Headquarters Washington
Discharge Given

NAME	RANK	REMARKS	LAST KNOWN P.O. ADDRESS
Albert B. Gordon	1st Lieut.		Middletown, NY
William A. Bennett	Sgt		Ithaca, NY
Philip A. Wever	"		
Samuel Mearns	"		Monticello, NY
Geo. B. VanOrman	Corporal		
George VanOrder	"		
Nelson S. White	"		
John Houghtaling	"		
Albert Bemant	"		
Cornelius B. Presonins	"		
Charles Randolph	"		
Aaron Poyer	"		Newfield, NY
Breitenbucher, Adam	Private		Roundout, NY
Conklin, Frank	"		
Cronce, William	"		
Curtis, Edward	"		
Collins, John	"		
Davis, James W.	"		
Doad, Reuben W.	"		
Frohlich, Clark	"		
Frohlich, Edwin	"		
Houghtaling, Sands R.	"	Died	
Holly, John C.	"		
Havens, Ansel B.	"		
Horace, Russell	"		
Longcoy, Harrison	"		Brooklyn, NY
Matthews, James H.	"		
Mallon, Barney	"		
McWilliams, Wesley	"		
Morgan, Chester S.	"		
Myers, George	"		
Norton, James	"		
Robbinson, David	"		
Stewart, James H.	"		Ithaca, NY
Stephens, Lewis	"		Ithaca, NY
Schryver, Chas. H.	"		
Slocum, Truxton	"		
Truce, George	"		
Troomev, Timothy	"		Ithaca, NY
Van Valkenburgh, Osa	"		
VanOrden, Moses	"		
Wood, Samuel	"		

ABSENT, NOT MUSTERED OUT WITH COMPANY

Lewis N. Stanton	Capt.	Died July 2, 1886
Denslow Hallady	Sgt.	
Theodore Deschner	"	
Cornelius, Horace	Private	
Coe, Henry	"	
Coe, Nelson	"	
Criddle, William H.	"	
Dickinson, John W.	"	
Depew, Elias G.	"	
Johnson, Norman C.	"	
Mitchell, Joseph	"	
Shaw, Henry	"	

DISCHARGED

John Higgins	Capt.	Promoted to Major.	Dead
C. Howell North	1st Lieut.		
Dewitt Apgar	"	45 William St, NY City	
John R. Groo	2nd Lieut.	158 W 120th St, NY City	
Jared Anderson	1st Sergt.		
James D. Egbert	Sergeant		
Linns S. Mackey	"		
Bickel, Adam	Priv.	Dec 22, 1862	
Burton, Charles	"	Jan 24, 1864	
Bishop, Jeremiah	"	Feb 16, 1863	
Francis, John	"	Dec 27, 1864	
Harrington, Stephen	"	Nov 26, 1863	
Jacob, Albert L.	"	July 1, 1865	
Layton, Chas. B.	"	July 16, 1865	
Mericle, VanGosbeck	"	April 16, 1863	
Piper, Jacob H.	"	Dec 9, 1862	
Pringle, John	"	Feb 27, 1863	
Price, Solomon	"	Feb 16, 1863	
Robbins, David B.	"	April 3, 1863	Perrysville, N.Y.
Snow, Will. G.	"	Feb 16, 1863	
Sturdevant, LeGrand	"	Sept 12, 1863	Dead

TRANSFERRED

DeWitt, Apgar	1st Sgt	Promoted to Sergeant Major
Asa A. Corkins	Corp.	Jan 16, 1864, V.R.C.
Dickinson, Willett	Priv.	To V.R.C.
Dunlavy, Dennis	"	"
Halliday, Adelbert	"	"
Hitchcock, William	"	"
Masten, Ahrm	"	"
Mead, Jacob	"	"
Norton, Will. H.	"	"
Patterson, John	"	"
Roberts, Francis W.	"	"

<u>DIED</u>

Luther G. Bunnel	Priv.	July 26, 1864 of wounds
John B. Gardner	"	Jan 25, 1863, typhoid fever
Charles W. Gust	"	Jan 30, 1863 "
William Holmes	"	July 16, 1863 Remittant fever
Carr, Jehial	"	Heart Disease
Horgin, Jefferson	"	July 27, 1863 Remittant fever
Loomis, Amon	Priv.	Sept 3, 1864, wounds
Morrison, Edward	"	Nov 1, 1863, chronic diarrhoea
Murphy, Edward	"	Railroad accident
Mix, Henry	"	July 14, 1864
Peck, John P.	"	Nov 20, 1863
Quick, DeWitt	"	Nov 28, 1864, diarrhoea
Reynolds, Sam'l M.	"	Oct 24, 1864. 1863. fever

<u>DESERTED</u>

Allen, David L.	Priv.	Oct 14, 1862	New York City
Berry, William	"	July 6, 1865	Elmira, NY
Champion, Wm.	"	Oct 14, 1862	New York City
Hendershot, Chas. W.	"	July 8, 1863	
Hibbard, George	"	Sept 1, 1862	Never mustered in to United States service.
Logan, Charles	"	Sept. 1, 1862	" " "
Lindsay, Chas. W.	"	July 19, 1863	
Osborne, Robert	"		
Roberts, John W.	"		

<u>MISSING</u>

Floran D. Ormsby	Corp.	Supposed to have been captured Oct 27, 1863

Co. "E" 143d N.Y.V. Infantry

Mustered out with the Company July 20th, 1865.
Special Order No. 160, Headquarters Washington
Discharge Given

NAME	RANK	REMARKS	LAST KNOWN P.O. ADDRESS
DeWitt Apgar	Captain		New York City
Chas. A. Smith	1st Lieut.		Monticello, NY
Foster F. Bennett	1st Sgt.		Meadville, PA
Zachariah Medler	Sergeant		Amsterdam, NY
Mortimer Race	Corporal		Equanock, PA
Hezekiah J. Reynolds	"		Hurleyville, NY
Elijah Schoonmaker	"		Port Jervis, NY
Hiram Adams	"		Glen Wild, NY
William Dunlap	"		
Lewis Skinner	"		
Robert Pollock	Wagoner		Wurtsboro, NY
Barber, Theodore	Private		Monticello, NY
Bowers, Edwin L.	"	Dead	
Breen, Charles L.	"		Barryville, NY
Clark, Elijah	"		Westbrookville, NY
Clark, Miles	"		"
Davis, William	"		
Graham, Samuel S.	"		Phillipsport, NY
Knapp, John L.	"		New York City
Masten, David W.	"		Newburgh, NY
Muir, David	"		Glen Wild, NY
McLaughlin, Henry C.	"		
McGovern, Patrick	"		Westbrookville, NY
Reed, Samuel	"		"
Skinner, Theodore	"		"
Scott, George W.	"		
Shaw, Levi	"		
Terwilliger, Aaron	"		
Tice, Horton	"		Amsterdam, NY
VanLuven, John	"		Ellenville, NY
Wade, Jacob S.	"		

ABSENT. NOT MUSTERED OUT WITH COMPANY

Austin A. Race	Sergeant		Bridgeville, NY
Jacob H. Sinsabaugh	Corporal		
Bennett, Jacob	Private		
DeGroot, Charles	"		Westbrookville, NY
Galloway, Marcus D.	"		
Gordon, James H.	"		Westbrookville, NY
Tarket, Levi W.	"		

DISCHARGED

Ira Dorrance	Capt.	March 1863	Middletown, NY
John F. Anderson	"	Feb 1, 1865	Callicoon Depot, NY
William R. Bennett	1st Lieut.	For promotion Nov 20, 1863	
Alexander H. Brown	1st Sgt	"	Nov 11, 1864
Philip D. Cole	Sgt	Sept 10, 1863	Westbrookville,NY
James B. Daved	Sgt	Dec 14, 1863	Phillipsport, NY
John Dunlap	Corp.	June 30, 1865	
Moses B. Cole	Musician Sept 20, 1863. Dead		
Benedict, Wm. F.	Priv.	June 15, 1864	Westbrookville,NY
Clemence, Benj. T.	"	May 20, 1864	Patterson, NY
Crawford, Charles N.	"	Aug 17, 1863	
Cuddington, James	"	June 28, 1865	Rock Hill, NY
Decker, Peter	"	June 28, 1865	Rock Hill, NY
Hoyt, Jonathan M.	"	Feb 27, 1864	Nineva, Broom, NY
Hawley, David S.	"	Apr 8, 1863	
Hardenburgh, Alexander	"	March 15, 1864	
Price, Henry R.	"	Jan 5, 1864	
Pierce, John W.	"	June 7, 1865	Westbrookville, NY
Skinner, Samuel L.	"	Feb 25, 1863	
Spencer, Elijah	"	May 24, 1863	
Smith, Charles A.	"	June 7, 1865	
Sarine, Ira	"	April 28, 1865	Summitville, NY
Tarket, DeWitt C.	"	Jan 12, 1863	
Tompkins, Daniel D.	"	March 14, 1863	
Tillson, Jesse	"	Oct 30, 1863	

TRANSFERRED

James A. Eickenburg	1st Sgt	Promoted to Sgt Major Warren,PA
Frantz, George C.	Priv.	To V.R.C.
Hardenburgh, John C.	"	To Hospital Stewart Phillipsport, NY
Simpson, Andrew J.	"	To V.R.C.
Skinner, Samuel W.	"	"
Sweet, John D.	"	"

DIED

Peter L. Waterbury	1st Lieut.	Of wounds received July 24, 1864 at Peach Tree Creek
Selar B. Decker	Corp.	May 15, 1864 killed in action at Resaca, Ga.
Adams, William	Priv.	March 25, 1865
Bennett, Isaac J.	"	March 19, 1865, killed at Bentonville, NC
Howard, George	"	Nov 19, 1863
Kniffen, James H.	"	Sept 7, 1864
Leonard, Levi	"	Feb 11, 1864
Nation, Joseph W.	"	Jan 1863
Pratt, John M.	"	June 22, 1862
Richard, John	"	June 16, 1868 Dead

```
St. John, Wm. J.          "    Jan 21, 1861
Skinner, Benj. A.         "    Oct 27, 1863
Sarine, Jacob             "    Of wounds in action.
Shaw, Thomas J.           "    Feb 3, 1864
Travisse, William         "    May 25, 1863. Killed in action.
Thompson, Jas. H.         "    July 11, 1863. Dead
VanLuven, Joachin H.      "    Jan 14, 1864
Whitmore, Andrew J.       "    Jan 1, 1864
Young, Matthew            "    Mar 18, 1863, committed suicide
```

DESERTED

```
Bishop, Chas.       Priv.  Nov 18, 1862
Bodle, William        "    Oct 9, 1862
Roover, John          "    Sept 28, 1863
Tompkins, Jehial C.   "    July 13, 1863    Walden, Orange
                                            Co., NY
```

Co. "F" 143d N.Y.V. Infantry
Mustered out with the Company July 20th, 1865.
Special Order No. 160, Headquarters Washington
Discharge Given

NAME	RANK	REMARKS	LAST KNOWN P.O. ADDRESS
Edward H. Pinney	Captain		Jeffersonville, NY
Dwight Divine	1ˢᵗ Lieut.		Ellenville, NY
George Anderson	1ˢᵗ Sergt.		Fremont Ctr, NY
David Fraser	Sergeant		
James S. Beattie	"		Rockland, NY
George Miller	"		Roscoe, NY
Henry Miller	Corporal		"
George Alber	"		Susquehanna, PA
James M. Benedict	"		Scranton, PA
George M. Swarthout	"		Owego, NY
Archibald H. Blackman	"		Fremont Ctr, NY
Geo. W. Parker	"		Eldred, NY
Francis H. Biffar	"		
Wm. H. Mitchell	"	Dead	
Jeremiah Bucksbee	Wagoner		New York City
Briner, John	Private		Callicoon, NY
Buri, Frederick	"	Dead	
Brady, Andrew	"		
Brown, William	"		Long Eddy, NY
Baird, Otis	"		
Cook, Enoch B.	"		Lanesboro, Pa
Davis, Joseph D.	"		Walton, NY
Ferdon, Anthony H.	"		Rockland, NY
Ferdon, John D.	"		
Gilbert, John	"		Callicoon, NY
Hill, Granger	"		Oscoda, Mich.
Hardie, Charles	"		
Hanser, Edward A.	"		Austen, PA
Hofer, John	"		New Haven, CT
Huff, Lewis	"		Jeffersonville, NY
Jacoby, Robert E.	"		
Sanab, Alfred	"		Binghamton, NY
Leib, Theodore	"		Scranton, PA
Mills, George H.	"		Liberty Falls, NY
Miller, John	"		Roscoe, NY
Priestley, John	"		Ralston, PA
Quick, Cyrus J.	"		North Branch, NY
Rose, James Jr.	"		Long Eddy, NY
Rose, William M.	"		North Branch, NY
Siebecker, Lewis	"		Scranton, PA
VonArr, Herman	"		English Ctr, PA
Williams, Henry H.	"		Great Bend, PA
Yowkee, Henry	"	Dead	

ABSENT, NOT MUSTERED OUT WITH COMPANY

Long, John	Private Dead	
Pendell, Sidney T.	"	Greenbush, NY
Rose, Caleb G.	"	Callicoon Depot, NY
Tremper, John	"	Portland Mills, PA

DISCHARGED

John F. Anderson	1st Lt. Nov 1, 1863 for promotion.
Franklin Buckley	2nd Lt. Mar 26, 1863, Special Order Middletown, NY
George H. Smith	Priv. Oct 8 1862 Dead
Alexander Jackson	" Dec 17 1862 Livingston Manor, NY
Chauncy Whitmarsh	" Dec 22 1862 Harrison, MO
William C. Smith	" Jan 2 1863 Dead
Rudolph VonArx	" Sep 5 1863 Jeffersonville NY
William S. Furdon	" Aug 29 1863
Herman Kimball	" Sep 22 1863 Peakville, NY
Willis Norton	" Dec 14 1863 Dead
Edward P. Smith	1st Sgt Jan 12 1864 Dead
Asa Cole	Priv. Feb 18 1864
Joseph Winslow	" Mar 11, 1864
George C. Pinney	1st Sgt For promotion Damascus, PA
Henry Coons	Priv. Bridgeville, NY
Chas. H. Hanford	"
John Norton	" Fremont Ctr, NY
George Murry	Sergeant
Alfred Wormouth	Private Butternut Grove, NY
John Wingart	"
Chas. Jackson	" Rockland, NY
Albert Gluckauf	"
Ulrich Huber	"
Orlando B. Fuller	" Dead
Ira F. Hitt	"
Lewis Hitt	"
Andrew J. Thompson	"
Nicholas Huber	"
Philip VanTassall	"
James A. Conklin	"
Stephen Wormouth	" Fosterdale, NY

TRANSFERRED

Marcus Maltby	Priv. Dead
Abrm Palmanteer	" Dead
Seth B. Mills	" White Sulphur Springs NY
L. B. Dusinberry	Sgt. Dead
James Walker	Priv. South Fallsburgh, NY
Edward J. Norton	Corp. Trout Brook, NY
Benj. Hartman	Priv. Dead
Lorenzo Albee	Corp. Rockland, NY
Wm. F. Morgans	1st Sgt Promotion, died after discharge
Lewis H. Short	Priv. New Haven, CT

DIED

Marcus Fraser	2nd Lt	Nov 20 1862	
Edward A. Lewis	Priv.	Jun 21 1863	
Isaac Wormouth	"	Jul 9 1863	
George Rumsey	"	Oct 18 1863	
George R. Misner	Corp.	Jul 25 1863	
Mark L. Williams	"	Nov 20 1863	
Albert Hector	Priv.	Nov 30 1863	
Eugene Edeline	"	Jan 6 1864	
John W. Reynolds	"	Dec 13 1863	
Cyrenus M. Fuller	"	Jan 6 1864	
Fillmore Hill	"	Jan 17 1864	
William Murray	"	May 26 1864,	of wounds
Clark J. Robertson	"	Jul 5 1864	
Andrew Hu-chen	"	Jul 20 1864,	killed in action
Aaron Hoaglen	1st Sgt	Jul 21 1864,	of wounds
George Miller	Priv.	Aug 28 1864	

DESERTED

Michael Ryan	Priv	Oct 13 1862
John Lynson	"	July 17 1863

Co. "G" 143d N.Y.V. Infantry
Mustered out with the Company July 20th, 1865.
Special Order No. 160, Headquarters Washington
Discharge Given

NAME	RANK	REMARKS	LAST KNOWN P.O. ADDRESS
Jeriah Young	Captain	Dead	
William T. Morgans	1st Sgt	Died at Middletown, NY	
Thomas DeLancy	Sergeant		Walton, NY
Levi Stewart	"		Parksville, NY
Paul P. Tice	"	Deceased	
Timothy Doolittle	Corp.	Deceased	
Andrew P. Budd	"		
Nathan M. Thomas	"		
Franklin Sturdevent	"		Kansas City, MO
Leonard Tompkins	"		Montgomery, NY
Alvah M. Chandler	"		Long Eddy, NY
Jeremiah Hazen	"		Bethel, NY
Chas. S. McWilliams	Musician		New York City
Allen Simpson	Private		
Billings, Philo	"		
Carpenter, Charles	"		
Cremar, Jeremiah	"		
Clark, Joseph W.	"		Susquehanna, PA
Cook, Mathias	"		Bloomingburgh, NY
Davis, Joseph	"		Walton, NY
Gould, Richard	"		
Gorton, Dubois	"		Sheffield, PA
Hull, Aaron B.	"		
Hosie, John P.	Private		
Kyrk, Ephraim E.	"		
Knapp, William	"		
Laning, Stephen	"		Warwick, NY
Kerr, Samuel	"		Long Eddy, NY
Odell, Jesse H.	"		Bloomingburgh, NY
Ousterhout, Geo. W.	"		
Robinson, William	"		Lew Beach, NY
Verwimp, John	"	Deceased	

ABSENT NOT TO BE MUSTERED OUT ON THIS ROLL

Peter Kellam	1st Sergt.		Equinunck, PA
Marvin Chandler	Sergeant		Fishes Eddy, NY
George S. Cain	Corp.	Deceased	
Boyle, Thomas E.	Priv.	Sergt 18 Bat. U.S. Engineer	New York City
Babcock, James H.	"		Middletown, NY
Bruster, Joel N.	"		
Baker, Chas. H.	"		Burlingham, NY
Hendrickson, Richard C	"		Swamp Mills, NY

Miller, Verdine H.   "   Middletown, NY
Warmsley, Warner   "   Deceased

DISCHARGED

Benj. Reynolds   Capt. Mar 7 1865   Parksville, NY
T. B. Luckley   1st Lt. Deceased
Rens Hammond   "   Aug 29 1864
A. C. Kellam   2d Lt Mar 17 1863
James H. Seaman   Sgt.   Deceased
Brown, James   Priv.   "   Sept 2, 1864
Dickinson, Marcelis   "
Davis, Prosper P.   "   Deceased
Krum, Peter L.   "   October 1863   Ellenville, NY
Meyers, John Jr.   "   June 14, 1864
Rockafellow, Ches. B.   "   June 2, 1865   Wurtsboro, NY
Seeley, Sanford L.   "   July 2, 1863   Deceased
Seeley, James L.   "   Jan. 7, 1865   Deceased
Tyler, William   "   June 6, 1865
Turner, Henry   "   May 17, 1865   Susquehanna, PA
Watts, Thomas   "   March 26, 1864 Deceased
Shields, Chas. J.   "   June 1865   Ellenville, NY
Reynolds, Wm. H.   "   July 1, 1865   Parksville, NY
Gorton, Joseph   "   June 1865
Lambert, Adam   "   "   "   Neversink, NY

TRANSFERRED

Babcock, George H.   Corp. To V.R.C., Deceased
Warner, Hughes   "   "   Rock Valley, NY
Achart, William, H.   Priv. "   Deceased
Bruster,   "   "   "   "
Warling, Stephen   Wagoner "   "
Conklin, George H.   Priv. "   "
Hawk, Christian   "   "
Kellem, Sandswirtte D. "   Equinunck, PA
Rose, George W.   Priv.
Todd, John   "

DECEASED

R.M.J. Hardenburgh   1st Lt. March 16, 1865 of wounds.
Dennis, Johnson   Sergeant " Killed in action.
Henry F. Fisher   Corp. Dec 8 1863
Brazer, Levi   Priv. March 4 1863
Kearney, Benjamin W.   "   Jan 27, 1864
Debens, James P.   "   Jan 1, 1864
Knapp, Nelson   "   Dec 18, 1863
Kimball, James   "   At Bridgeport, Ala., date unknown
Milligan, William G.   "   Jan 5 1864
Rose, William E.   "   Jan 12 1864
Ryder, Jacob T.   "   Jan 30 1863
Reynolds, Hiram T.   "   At Jeffersonville, date unknown

Scott, Adam	"	Nov 10 1863
Turner, Nathaniel	"	Dec 20 1863
Teller, Horace D.	"	Oct 30 1862 of wounds at Look Out Valley, Tenn.
Walker, John Jacob	"	Oct 7 1864

DESERTED

William V. Luckey	Sgt.	Aug 26 1864	Middletown, NY
Louesi, Marianna	Priv.	March 12, 1863	
Watts, Thomas	"	July 11 1863	Deceased
Hutchins, Chester D.	"	July 16, 1863	Deceased
Billings, Philo C	"	July 1863	

Co. "H" 143d N.Y.V. Infantry

Mustered out with the Company July 20th, 1865.
Special Order No. 160, Headquarters Washington
Discharge Given

NAME	RANK	REMARKS	LAST KNOWN P.O. ADDRESS
George H. Decker	Capt	Died at Liberty, NY	
George C. Pinney	1st Lt.		Damascus, PA
William Stoddard	Sergeant		
Harry Ward	"		Circleville, NY
William Cole, Jr.	Corporal		Ridgeville, PA
Matthew Decker	"		Willowemoc, NY
William D. Annis	"		Parksville, NY
Andrew Murry	"		Sheffield, PA
John H. Grant	"		Liberty, NY
John Caulkins	"		Liberty, NY
Brace, Isaac	Private		Greenfield
Barnhart, Stephen C.	"	Dead	
Bradley, Walter	"		Brooklyn, NY
Burton, George W.	"		Petries Corners, Lewis County, NY
Barker, Edward	Priv.		Livingston Manor, NY
Caulkins, George H.	"		Monticello, NY
Conklin, Levi	"		Mongaup Valley NY
Campbell, Benj. F.	"		Ridgeway, PA
Conklin, Mannings	"		Lew Beach, NY
Clark, George	"		Knoxville, Tenn
Cochran, Archibald	"		Livingston Manor, NY
Dawson, David L.	"		
Decker, Gideon W.	"		Willowemoc, NY
Dudley, Aaron	"		"
Doran, James	"		
Ellis, George M.	"		Galeton, PA
Gillett, Luther W.	"		
Grant, Lewis	"		Parksville, NY
Havens, Samuel H.	"		
Kniffen, Benjamin	"		
Layman, Alston	"		
Lewis, Joseph P.	"		Parksville, NY
Lewis, Samuel A.	"		Glen Wild, Ny
Marvin, John B.	"		
Morse, John W.	"		Maplewood, NY
Maffitt, Ferris	"		
McKellip, Enos C.	"		Rolfe, PA
Porter, Orson	"		Union, NJ
Rose, Gustavus	"		
Roosa, William M.	"		Liberty, Ny
Rose, Garrett	"		Livingston Manor, NY
Rose, Hiram E.	"		Churchill, Mich.

Shafer, Jacob E.	Priv.	
Sprague, Lafayette	"	Livingston Manor, NY
Winner, Solomon	"	Emmonsville, NY
Whipple, Chas. C.	"	Emmonsville, NY
Ward, Joseph	"	Livingston Manor, NY

ABSENT NOT MUSTERED OUT WITH COMPANY

Rufus W. Porter	1st Sergeant	Main, Brown Co., NY
Chauncey S. Fisk	Sergeant	Plainview, Minn.
Jerry Crary	"	Sheffield, PA
Jonathan French	Corporal	Mongaup Valley NY
Eber C. Young	"	'
Borden, Hiram	Private	Churchill, Mich.
Clark, William H.	"	
Campbell, William H.	"	
Collins, Thomas D.	"	Livingston Manor, NY
Conklin, David A.	"	
Irons, George H.	"	Hurleyville, NY
McPhillemy, Robert	"	
Parliman, William H.	"	
Travis, Chas. W.	"	Sheldreke, NY
Warring, Graham	"	Sheffield, PA
Woodward, Archibald	"	

DISCHARGED

Jirah J. Young	1st Lt	June 19, 1865,	promotion, Dead
Rensslaer Hammond	2d Lt	May 1, 1864	Lansing, Kansas
Alexander H. Brown	"	May 15, 1865	
Erastus D. Beach	Serg.	March 9, 1863	
William J. Gerow	"	March 7, 1864	Liberty, NY
Andrew J. Stickles	Corp.	May 27, 1865	Coudersport, PA
Armstrong, Stephen	Priv.	General Order	DeBruce, NY
Benson, Garrett W.	"	" "	Grahamsville, NY
Benton, James H.	"	" "	
Barnhart, George	"	" "	
Beach, Hiram	"	Feb 17, 1864	
Curry, Richard C.	"	General Order	
Carrier, Adelbert A.	"	May 18, 1865	
Donaldson, Cornelius	"	General Order	
Drennon, Robert	"	March 13, 1863	Liberty, NY
Eckert, Augustus O.	"	General Order	Grahamsville, NY
French, William H.	"	May 19, 1863	Harvard, NY
Farce, William	"	General Order	
Gorton, William	"	" "	Grahamsville, NY
Howard, John M.	Wagoner	Aug 8, 1863	Stone Ridge, NY
Hill, George	Priv.	July 30, 1864	Dead
Lair, James D.	"	General Order	
Hector, Hiram	"	June 17, 1865	
Huntington, Edward H.	"	June 6, 1865	
Lewis, Chas. W.	"	July 1 1865	Liberty, NY
Murry, Adolphus, E.	"	Nov 21, 1863	Burnwood, NY
Porter, Henry W.	"	Sept 29, 1864	

Rose, Seth B.   Priv. General Order Churchville, Mich
Sheeley, Calvin   "   "   "   Ellenville, NY
Slater, Stephen   "   "   "   Grahamsville, NY
Sherwood, Roswell, F.   "   Aug 17, 1863 Dead
Smith, William J.   "   July 7, 1865
Wager, Enos   "   Sept 12, 1863
Gray, Benj.   "   Sept 13, 1863 Cooks Falls, NY

TRANSFERRED

Hamelton, William   Priv. 1863 Gen. Order, Dening, NY
Decker, John D. W.   "   "   "   Livingston Manor, NY
Gildersleve, John A.   "   "   "   Liberty Falls, NY
Morgan, Patrick   "   Vet. Res. 1864 Liberty, NY
Young, Robert   "   "   "   "

DIED

Beasmer, DeWitt C.   Priv. Nov 2, 1863, Nashville, Tenn
Atwell, Selah   "   July 22 1864, wounded in action
Chapman, Amos M.   "   July 27 1864   "   "   "
Decker, William   "   Dec 13 1863, Lookout Valley, TN
Ellis, Sirel   "   Dec 21, 1863,   "   "   "
Edwards, James H.   "   Dec 20, 1863, Liberty, NY
Foster, Moses H.   "   Nov 10, 1863, Stevenson, Ala.
Falkerson, Seymour J.   "   July 21 1864, wounded in action
Osterhout, Gideon   "   Nov 2 1863, Nashville, Tenn.
Chas. G. Reese   Corp. Feb 19, 1865

DESERTED

Baker, Anthon   Priv. Oct 14, 1862
Campbell, Wm. H.   "   Sept 2, 1862, released by
                                         special order.
Hodge, Leander A.   "   April 2, 1863
Kile, George W.   "
McLynn, James   "   Never reported to Company.
O'Brian, John   "   "   "   "   "
Whitmarsh, Sanford   "   Oct 14, 1862

Co. "I" 143d N.Y.V. Infantry

Mustered out with the Company July 20th, 1865.
Special Order No. 160, Headquarters Washington
Discharge Given

NAME	RANK	REMARKS	LAST KNOWN P.O. ADDRESS
Harrison, Marvin	Captain		Albany, NY
Wallace Hill	1st Lieut.		Scranton, PA
Elihu Hilderbrant	1st Sergt.		Buffalo, NY
William McRoe	Sergeant		Etna, NY
Otis A. Bates	"		McLean, NY
Langton Robinson	"	Died at Dryden, NY	
Bielby P. Starr	Corporal	Unknown	
Daniel D. Davenport	"	Died at Orange, NY	
Arnold Chiddiah	Private		Rathboneville, NY
Baldwin, William	"		Elmira, NY
Ballard, Gabriel R.	"		Rochester, NY
Dodge, Levi	"		
Donahoe, Patrick	"		
Edsall, William	"		Dryden, NY
Fahunking, John F.	"		
Nash, David	"		Hartford, NY
Peas, Almond	"		Cortland, NY
Rizir, Jacob	"		
Ryder, William	"		Syracuse, NY
Smith, Thomas	"		
Sutton, John S.	"		
Shave, John W.	"		Freeville, NY
Tanner, Garrett	"		
Wait, Henry B.	"		Etna, NY
Wickham, George	"		Dryden, NY

ABSENT NOT MUSTERED OUT WITH COMPANY

Frank Jugger	Corporal	Dead
George Woodmancy	"	"
Chambers, Amos	"	Died at Slaterville, NY
Fogerty, John	"	Dead

DISCHARGED

William T. George	1st Lt	Promoted to Captain,	Company A.
William S. Moffat	2d Lt	" " 1st Lt,	Company D.
Henry H. Hemingway	1st Sgt	" " " ",	Company C.
John T. McWhorter	Serg	July 11, 1864	
Peter Seaman	"	May 16, 1865	White Church, NY
Gilbert Devanny	"	Dec 24, 1864	Dead
Daniel Hollinshead	Corp.	Jan 28, 1863	Catteraugus, NY
Brigham, Newton	Priv.	Dec 29, 1862	
Brown, Arson C.	"	Aug 27, 1864	Ithaca, NY

Billington, George	Priv.	Apr 11, 1863	West Dryden, NY
Cole, Robert	"	Apr 1, 1864	
Ferris, John J.	"	Jan 18, 1863	
Fox, Merritt B.	"	Aug 26, 1863	Dead
Fisher, Willet	"	Jun 23, 1865	
Hulslander, William	"	Dec 31, 1862	
Harviland, Albert	"	Apr 17, 1863	
How, James T.	"	Sept 1 1863	Dead
Hemmingway, Chauncy	"	June 19, 1865	Dead
Hathaway, Wm. H.	"	July 3, 1865	
Hayes, Michael	"	July 3, 1865	
Knickerbocker, Clay E.	"	Dec 22, 1862	Owego, NY
Lambesson, Wm.	"	Apr 2 1863 Dead	
Lambesson, James E.	"	Aug 26, 1863	New Mexico
Perrigo, Chas M.	"	Sept 17, 1863	Auburn, NY
Payne, John	"	Jul 20, 1863	
Punderbaugh, Theodore	"	July 3, 1865	Dead
Skillmore, James M.	"	Apr 30, 1863	
Sherwood, John	"	" " "	Dead
Snyder, Henry J.	"	Apr 1, 1864	
Shaw, Henry	"	June 1865	
Terwilliger, Chas. O.	"	June 7, 1865	Dead
Wait, Andrew	"	Dec 12, 1862	Etna, NY
Ward, Al	"	Jan 28, 1863	

TRANSFERRED

John W. Copley	1st Sgt Vet. Res.	Sept 1, 1863
Elisha Hurley	Corp. " "	March 15, 1864 Dead
Hurd, John	Priv. " "	Sept 1, 1863
		Brooklyn, NY
Watson, John C.	" " "	1863, Dead
Maxwell, Edward	" " "	July 1 1863
		Dryden, NY
Wilson, Edward B.	" " "	Aug 10 1864
		Eldred, NY

DIED

Bloomfield, Edward	Priv.	Feb 14 1864 Murfreesboro, TN
Besser, Peter	"	Feb 27 1864 Louisville, KY
Conklin, Harrison	"	May 19 1865 wounds resica.
Cook, Enis	"	Dec 18 1863 Lookout Valley, TN
Duel, James M.	"	Mar 25 1863 Alexandria, VA
Decker, Rufus	"	Aug 14 1864 Nashville, TN
Fitts, Henry W.	"	Jan 11 1864 Lookout Valley, TN
Hartsough, Thomas	Corp.	Dec 6 1863 Lookout Valley, TN
Harned, George	Priv.	Sept 28 1863 Fort Monroe, VA
Hemmingway, Orlando	Sergt.	Oct 15 1863 Alexandria, VA
Kizer, Albert	Priv.	Sept 1 1864 wounded in action
Mosher, Philip	"	Jan 11 1863 Alexandria, VA
Morey, William A.	"	June 25 1864 Chattanooga, TN
Overacker, Isaac	"	Apr 4 1864 Dryden, NY
Pattergill, Florel	Corp.	Dec 5 1862 Washington, D.C.
Scutt, Socrates	Priv.	Apr 6 1863 "

```
Sherwood, Wm. P.      Priv.  Nov 4 1863 Bridgeport, Ala.
Sherwood, Morgan        "    Nov 15 1863 Nashville, TN
Smith, Lawrence         "    July 30 1864 killed in action
                                        at Atlanta, GA.
```

DESERTED

```
Armstrong, Thomas     Priv.  June 22 1865
Coykendall, Harrison    "      "    "    "
Campbell, John          "    June 9 1865
Ferris, David           "    Oct 14, 1862
Farrell, Andrew         "         "
McDermott, James      Corp.  Sep 29 1862
Nugent, John          Priv.       "         Dryden, NY
Pratt, Samuel           "    Apr 29 1863
Shaw, William           "    Oct 11 1862
Swain, William H.       "    June 25 1865
Tomlinson, Robt.        "    Sept 29 1862
Tompkins, Nicholas      "    Apr 15 1863    Dead
Welsh, James            "    Sept 29 1862   Dryden, NY
Wait, James             "    Oct 9 1862     Coonrod, NY
Wright, George W.       "    Oct 9 1862     Canada
Willcox, Lyman          "    Oct 14 1862
```

MISSING

```
Freeman, Chas. D.     Priv.  Missing since Nov 28 1863,
                             supposed to be dead.
```

Co. "K" 143d N.Y.V. Infantry
Mustered out with the Company July 20th, 1865.

Mustered out with the Company July 20th, 1865.
Special Order No. 160, Headquarters Washington
Discharge Given

NAME	RANK	REMARKS	LAST KNOWN P.O. ADDRESS
Peter E. Palen	1st Lieut.		Monticello, NY
Daniel A. Bedford	1st Sergt.		Narrowsburgh, NY
Paul Marold	Sergeant		Damascus, PA
Wesley J. Woodruff	"		Newark, NJ
Wallace Keesler	Corporal		Damascus, PA
Chas. B. Layton	"		Callicoon Depot NY
James R Calkins	"		"
George W. Davenport	"		Barryville, NY
Wm H Hill	Musician		Rowlands, PA
Arch Eaberhart	Private		
Brining, James	"		Binghamton, NY
Bamper, Garrett L.	"		
Baird, Andrew J.	"	Dead	
Connell, Patrick	"	Dead	
Conner, Patrick J.	"		Callicoon Depot NY
Conklin, Wm.	"	Dead	
Detrick, John M.	"		Port Jervis, NY
Dexter, Benj. D.	"		Narrowsburgh, NY
Fagan, John	"		Scranton, PA
Hill, James	"		
Keesler, Solomon	"		Cochecton Ctr, NY
Lent, Thomas O.	"		Warren County, PA
Lent, Charles	"		Hankins, NY
Lillie, Harrison	"		Bethel, NY
Marold, Robert	"		Narrowsburgh, NY
Miller, Lewis H	"		
McGusy, Matthew	"		Coudersport, PA
Morris, John	"		
Osterhout, Cornelius	"		
Perry, George	"		
Pendergrass, John	"		Monticello, NY
Sutton, Adolphus	"		
Swalm, Lewis	"		12 Union Square, NY City
Tyler, William	"		Cochecton Ctr, NY
VanWagnon, Herman	"		

ABSENT NOT MUSTERED OUT WITH COMPANY

Willett T. Embler	2d Lieut.	Discharge given at Harts Island, NY July 25, 1892 New York City
John Akins	Corporal	Callicoon, NY
Michael Beesmer	"	
Dodge, Cyrenus	Private	

Ellery, John	Priv.	Dead	
Foster, John A.	"	Dead	
Goff, Nathan	"		Mongaup Valley NY
Hill, Elias B.	"		
Hendrickson, Jon. H.	"		Scranton, PA
Lent, Joseph A.	"		Equinock, PA
Powell, Joseph	"		New York City
Skinner, Weston D.	"		Milwaukee, PA
Stahl, John	"		
Wallestine, Lewis	"		
Williams, Burroughs	"		

DISCHARGED

Anthony H. Bush	Capt.	Mar 31 1863 order of Court Martial.
C. Howell North	"	July 15 1864
Lewis N. Stanton	1st Lt.	Apr 30 1864 promoted to Capt., Company D. died June 2 1886 at Narrowsburgh, NY
John B. Saunders	Priv	Jan 4 1863 Carlisle, PA
Lawrence Detrick	Priv.	Apr 2 1863
John H. Wheeler	"	Aug 26 1864
James Sackett	"	Sept 8 1863 Grahamsville, NY
Henry Urben	"	Mar 16 1863
Newton Cornish	"	Dec 29 1862
Chris Bauernfiend	"	Feb 1 1863 Dead
Isaac Jelliff	1st Sgt	Apr 30 1864 promoted to Co. B
Albert B. Gordon	"	Apr 25 1865 promoted to Co. D
Augustus H. Keesler	Priv.	May 26 1865
William O Laden	"	May 26 1865
Joshua H. Quick	"	May 3 1865

TRANSFERRED

John H. Barrett	Priv.	Vet Res Sept 1 1863
James Vantrum	"	" Apr 10 1864 Woodbourne NY
John H. Mason	"	" March 31 1864
Chas. Guinnipp	"	" Jan 10 1864
Edward O. Green	Sergt.	" Apr 1 1865 Narrowsburgh NY

DIED

Albert W. Chittenden	Sergt	May 1 1863 Chesepeak Hospital
William C Bentley	Priv	Jun 18 1863 Yorktown, VA
Henry J Lent	Corp.	Jun 18 1863 Yorktown, VA
George Tracy	"	Nov 24 1863 Nashville, TN
John L Knapp	"	Dec 25, 1863 Lookout Valley, TN
George L. Decker	Priv.	Nov 28 1863 New Albany, Ind.
Elias Hendrickson	"	Nov 23 1863 Nashville, TN
Peter Ellry	"	Dec 20 1863 Chattanooga, TN
John G. Ross	"	Nov 3 1863 Stevenson, Ala.
Jerome Wood	"	Nov 13 1863 Nashville, TN
Gilbert Apply	"	Jan 2 1864 Lookout Valley, TN

Aaron Hoffman	Priv.	Jan 2 1864 Murfreysboro, TN
Walter Ingric	"	Jan 3 1864 Lookout Valley, TN
William H Smith	"	Apr 5 1864 Murfreysboro, TN
Daniel L. Dibble	"	Killed in action July 20 1864
Conrad Keesler	"	Oct 3 1864 Chattanooga, TN
Clinton A Baird	Sergt.	Apr 16 1865 of wounds
Augustus Harre	Priv.	Aug 18 1864 Andersonville, GA
Benjamin Boultz	Wagoner	May 22 1862 Hospital

DESERTED

Richard Angel	Priv.	Oct 14 1862
Stephen Funda	"	Oct 8 1862
John Hickey	"	Feb 28 1863
Lamando Tyler	"	Jan 1863
John J. Quick	"	Sept 24 1863
Geo W. Van Wert	"	Dropped as a deserter Apr 9 1865, not heard from Feb 30 1864
Amos Lee	"	Dec 21 1863 while on duty.
Nicholas Elbert	"	Left sick July 14 1863, never heard from after.
Wm. H. Osterhout	"	Dropped Apr 21 1866 as deserter
Thomas Murry	"	June 2 1865.

MISSING IN ACTION

Isaac F. Tuttle	Priv.	Nov 29 1863
Philip Mock	"	Nov 19 1864

(Compiled and published Oct. 1, 1892)

SUMMARY OF CONSTITUTION AND BY-LAWS.

1st. The association shall be known as the survivors of the 143d Regt. N.Y. Inft. Vols.

2d. All honorably discharged officers and soldiers are eligible to membership and to hold office therein.

3d. The object is to continue that spirit of loyalty and fidelity to country that brought us together; to perpetuate its principles; to collect facts and make a record of the same, and to establish and maintain a complete roster of the regiment.

4th. Political and other discussions foreign to the object of the association prohibited.

5th. Meets annually Oct. 10th. Unless that day comes on Saturday, Sunday or Monday, when it will meet on the Tuesday following. The place of meeting fixed by vote of association at business meeting.

6th. Officers: A President, 1st and 2d Vice-Presidents, Secretary, and Treasurer elected annually.

7th. The President shall preside at all meetings and shall give at least two weeks notice of all meetings in the papers and secure reduced rates to meetings when he can.

8th. The Vice-Presidents possess powers of President in his absence.

9th. The Secretary shall keep minutes of all meetings, and shall be the corresponding Secretary of the Association.

10th. The Treasurer shall give a bond – the amount to be fixed by the association; receive and pay all moneys, and report at each annual meeting.

11th. Members elected by 2/3 vote at annual meetings.

12th. Any member may be expelled by 2/3 vote of any annual meeting for conduct unbecoming a soldier and a gentleman, of which the association shall be the judge; the accused to have notice and opportunity to defend himself.

13th. Cushing's Manual shall govern all meetings.

14th. The annual dues, fixed at twenty-five cents subject to change by 2/3 vote; members in arrears not entitled to vote.

15th. All standing resolutions considered By-Laws and to be recorded between the Constitution and minutes.

16th. The Constitution and By-Laws amended by majority vote, a notice of the amendment having been given at the preceding annual meeting.

143rd REGT. INDEX

Surname	First	Initial	Page
Achart	William	H.	34
Adams	Hiram		27
Adams	William		28
Akins	Amos	P.	17
Akins	George	H.	15
Akins	John		42
Albee	Lorenzo		31
Alber	George		30
Alberly	Thomas		17
Allen	Archibald	C.	15
Allen	David	L.	26
Allen	John	M.	16
Allen	Seymour	R.	16
Allen	William	C.	16
Allyn	Benjamin	F.	18
Anderson	George		30
Anderson	Jared		25
Anderson	John	F.	31
Anderson	John	F.	28
Angel	Richard		44
Annis	William	D.	36
Apgar	DeWitt		27
Apgar	DeWitt		25
Apgar	Dewitt		25
Apgar	DeWitt		16
Apgar	DeWitt		14
Apgar	Edgar	K.	13
Apply	Gilbert		43
Armstron	Stephen		37
Armstrong	Thomas		41
Ashton	William	H.	15
Atwell	George		22
Atwell	Selah		38
Avery	William	L.	19
Babcock	George	H.	34
Babcock	James	H.	33
Baily	Charles	A.	15
Baird	Andrew	J.	42
Baird	Clinton	A.	44
Baird	Otis		30
Baker	Anthony		38
Baker	Chas.	H.	33
Baker	David	B.	15
Baldwin	Alfred	J.	19
Baldwin	William		39
Ballard	Gabriel	R.	39
Bamper	Garrett	L	42

Surname	First	Initial	Page
Barber	Theodore		27
Barker	Edward		36
Barkley	Anthony		23
Barnhart	George		37
Barnhart	Herman		23
Barnhart	Stephen	C.	36
Barnhart	Wm.		22
Barrett	John	H.	43
Bates	Benjamin		18
Bates	Otis	A.	39
Bates	Thomas		15
Bauernfiend	Chris.		43
Beach	Erastus	D.	37
Beach	Hiram		37
Beasmer	DeWitt	C.	38
Beattie	James	S.	30
Bedford	Daniel	A.	42
Beebe	Joseph	L.	17
Beebe	Roswell	T.	16
Beesmer	Michael		42
Bemant	Albert		24
Benedict	James	M.	30
Benedict	Wm.	F.	28
Bennett	Asa	A.	22
Bennett	Foster	F.	27
Bennett	Isaac	J.	28
Bennett	Jacob		27
Bennett	Miller	P.	22
Bennett	William	R.	28
Bennett	William	A.	24
Bennett	William	R.	21
Bennett	William		17
Benson	Garrett	W.	37
Bentley	William	C.	43
Benton	James	H.	37
Berry	William		26
Besser	Peter		40
Bickel	Adam		25
Biffar	Francis	H.	30
Billings	Philo	C.	35
Billings	Philo		33
Billington	George		40
Biship	Jeremiah		25
Bishop	Chas.		29
Black	James	A.	23
Black	John		18
Black	John		16
Blackman	Archibald	H.	30
Bloemingburgh	Wm.	J.	19
Bloomfield	Edward		40
Bodle	William		29
Bolhman	Christopher		18
Bollman	Christopher	S.	20

Surname	First	Initial	Page
Borden	Hiram		37
Boughton	Horace		13
Boultz	Benjamin		44
Bowers	Alfred		21
Bowers	Edwin	L.	27
Bowers	Herman		23
Bowers	Palmer		22
Bowman	Melchoir		19
Boyle	Thomas	E.	33
Brace	Isaac		36
Bradley	Walter		36
Brady	Andrew		30
Brazer	Levi		34
Breen	Charles	L.	27
Breitenbucher	Adam		24
Briggs	William	A.	21
Brigham	Newton		39
Briner	John		30
Brining	James		42
Brodhead	Uriah	M.	18
Brown	Albert	N.	21
Brown	Albert		15
Brown	Alexander	H.	37
Brown	Alexander	H.	28
Brown	Arson	C.	39
Brown	James		34
Brown	James	L	15
Brown	Leander	T.	19
Brown	Marcus	L.	19
Brown	Orvil	A.	20
Brown	Renwick		18
Brown	William		30
Brown	William	B.	21
Bruster	Joel	N.	33
Bruster	William		34
Buckley	Franklin		31
Buckley	Philo		16
Bucksbee	Jeremiah		30
Budd	Andrew	P.	33
Bunnel	Luther	G.	26
Buri	Frederick		30
Burns	Frederick	W.	16
Burton	Charles		25
Burton	George	W.	36
Bush	Anthony	H.	43
Cain	George	S.	33
Calkins	James	R.	42
Cammer	Joseph		15
Campbell	Benj.	F.	36
Campbell	John		41
Campbell	William	H.	37
Campbell	Wm.	H.	38
Cantine	Nicholas	S.	19

Surname	First	Initial	Page
Cantrell	Edward	R.	16
Cantrell	John		15
Cantrell	Robert		18
Cantrell	Thomas		15
Carpenter	Benjamin		20
Carpenter	Charles		33
Carpenter	John	W.	17
Carpenter	Will.	L.	20
Carr	Jehial		26
Carrier	Adelbert	A.	37
Carrington	Edward		19
Carroll	Orrin	A.	13
Casterline	Edward		15
Caulkins	George	H.	36
Caulkins	John		36
Cauthers	Henry	A.	21
Chambers	Amos		39
Champion	Wm.		26
Chandler	Alvah	M.	33
Chandler	Marvin		33
Chapman	Amos	M.	38
Chapman	Jones		22
Chiddiah	Arnold		39
Chittenden	Albert	W.	43
Clark	Elijah		27
Clark	Garrett	T.	19
Clark	George		36
Clark	Joseph	W.	33
Clark	Miles		27
Clark	Nathaniel	C.	22
Clark	William	H.	37
Clemence	Benj.	T.	28
Cochran	Archibald		36
Coddington	Abner	J.	21
Coddington	Monroe		21
Coe	Henry		25
Coe	Nelson		25
Cogswell	Richard		20
Cole	Asa		31
Cole	Moses	B.	28
Cole	Philip	D.	28
Cole	Robert		40
Cole	William	Jr.	36
Coleman	Henry	B.	16
Collins	John		24
Collins	Thomas	D.	37
Conklin	Benjamin		21
Conklin	David	A.	37
Conklin	Eugene		18
Conklin	Frank		24
Conklin	George	H.	34
Conklin	Harrison		40
Conklin	James	A.	31

Surname	First	Initial	Page
Conklin	Levi		36
Conklin	Mannings		36
Conklin	Theodore		22
Conklin	Wm.		42
Connell	Patrick		42
Conner	Patrick	J.	42
Conor	Thomas	A.	15
Cook	Enis		40
Cook	Enoch	B.	30
Cook	Mathias		33
Coons	Henry		31
Copley	John	W.	40
Corby	Orrin	B.	15
Corgal	Thomas		15
Corkins	Asa	A.	25
Cornelius	Horace		25
Cornish	Newton		43
Cox	Abraham		15
Cox	Joseph	E.	22
Coykendall	Harrison		41
Craft	Herman		13
Crary	Jerry		37
Crawford	Charles	N.	28
Cremar	Jeremiah		33
Criddle	William	H.	25
Cromwell	Alexander		18
Cronce	William		24
Crosby	Scipio	L.	18
Cross	Cornelius		21
Cross	George	W.	22
Cuddington	James		28
Cumfort	Rieve		19
Curry	Richard	C.	37
Curtis	Edward		24
Darbee	Cleveland		22
Darbee	John	A.	22
Darbee	John	W.	21
Darling	David		16
Daved	James	B.	28
Davenport	Daniel	D.	39
Davenport	George	W.	42
Davis	James	W.	24
Davis	Joseph		33
Davis	Joseph	D.	30
Davis	Prosper	P.	34
Davis	William		27
Dawson	David	L.	36
Debens	James	P.	34
Decker	Chas.	H.D.	18
Decker	George	L.	43
Decker	George	H.	36
Decker	Gideon	W.	36
Decker	John	D.W.	38

Surname	First	Initial	Page
Decker	Matthew		36
Decker	Peter		28
Decker	Rufus		40
Decker	Selar	B.	28
Decker	William		38
Decker	William	N.	16
DeGroot	Charles		27
DeKay	James	C.	21
DeLancy	Thomas		33
Demerest	Jonathan	O.	20
Demunn	Francis	M.	23
Dennis	William		22
Denniston	John	G.	21
Depew	Elias	G.	25
Deschner	Theodore		25
Detrick	John	M.	42
Detrick	Lawrence		43
Devanny	Gilbert		39
DeWitt	David	P.	13
Dewitt	John		23
Dexter	Benj.	D.	42
Dibble	Daniel	L.	44
Dice	Henry		16
Dickinson	John	W.	25
Dickinson	Marcelis		34
Dickinson	Willett		25
Divine	Dwight		30
Divine	Dwight		22
Doad	Reuben	W.	24
Dobbs	Michael		17
Dodge	Cyrenus		42
Dodge	Cyrus		17
Dodge	Levi		39
Dodge	McKendru	N.	21
Doloway	Stephen	L.	21
Donahoe	Patrick		39
Donaldson	Cornelius		37
Donaldson	John	B.	23
Doolittle	Timothy		33
Doran	James		36
Dorrance	Ira		28
Drennon	Robert		37
Drennon	Robert		16
Dudley	Aaron		36
Duel	James	M.	40
Dunlap	John		28
Dunlap	William		27
Dunlavy	Dennis		25
Dunn	Summer	H.	18
Durland	James		19
Durland	Stephen	D.	20
Dusinberry	L.	B.	31
Eaberhart	Arch.		42

Surname	First	Initial	Page
Earnest	Adam		18
Eberlin	Henry		21
Eckert	Augustus	O.	37
Edeline	Eugene		32
Edsall	Henry	M.	13
Edsall	William		39
Edwards	James	H.	38
Egbert	James	D.	25
Eickenbergh	Jas.	A.	13
Eickenburg	James	A.	28
Elbert	Nicholas		44
Eldridge	George	D.	15
Ellery	John		43
Ellis	George	M.	36
Ellis	Sirel		38
Ellry	Peter		43
Elmore	Bruce		21
Elmore	Willard		21
Embler	Willett	T.	42
Everard	Eleasor		16
Everdon	Edwin	J.	17
Everett	George	H.	22
Fagan	John		42
Fahunking	John	F.	39
Falkerson	Seymour	J.	38
Farce	William		37
Farrell	Andrew		41
Ferdon	Anthony	H.	30
Ferdon	Anthony	C.	23
Ferdon	John	D.	30
Ferguson	James		18
Ferris	David		41
Ferris	John	J.	40
Finch	Isaac	N.	22
Fincle	William		21
Fisher	Herny	F.	34
Fisher	Ira		19
Fisher	Peter	A.	16
Fisher	William	J.	16
Fisher	Willlet		40
Fisk	Chauncey	S.	37
Fitts	Henry	W.	40
Fitzgerald	James		20
Fogerty	John		39
Foot	Edward	F.	16
Foot	Shubal		18
Foster	John	A.	43
Foster	John	A.	14
Foster	Moses	H.	38
Fox	Merritt	B.	40
France	Isaac	C.	18
Francis	John		25
Frantz	George	C.	28

Surname	First	Initial	Page
Fraser	David		30
Fraser	Marcus		32
Frasier	Will.	J.	20
Fredmore	Abrm.	S.	19
Freeman	Chas.	D.	41
Freeman	Dan	M.	19
French	James	C.	22
French	Jonathan		37
French	William	H.	37
Frohlich	Clark		24
Frohlich	Edwin		24
Fuller	Cyrenus	M.	32
Fuller	Orlando	B.	31
Funda	Stephen		44
Furch	George		21
Furdon	William	S.	31
Galloway	Marchus	B.	27
Gardener	Austin		21
Gardner	John	B.	26
Geary	Dan		18
George	William	T.	15
George	William	T.	39
Gerow	William	J.	37
Gilbert	Isaac		13
Gilbert	John		30
Gildersleve	John	A.	38
Gillett	Luther	W.	36
Gluckauf	Albert		31
Goff	Nathan		43
Gordon	Albert	B.	43
Gordon	Alfred	B.	24
Gordon	James	H.	27
Gorton	Dubois		33
Gorton	James	D.	21
Gorton	John	T.	21
Gorton	Joseph		34
Gorton	Nelson		23
Gorton	William		37
Gould	Richard		33
Graham	Samual	S.	27
Grant	John	H.	36
Grant	Lewis		36
Gray	Benj.		38
Green	Edward	O.	43
Gregory	Stephen	P.	16
Gregory	Stephen	J.	15
Groo	John	R.	25
Groo	John	R.	22
Guinnipp	Chas.		43
Gust	Charles	W.	26
Hadden	James	H.	17
Haight	Walter	T.	15
Haines	George	N.	19

Surname	First	Initial	Page
Hallady	Denslow		25
Halliday	Adelbert		25
Hamelton	William		38
Hammond	Rens		34
Hammond	Rensselaer		13
Hammond	Rensselear		37
Hanford	Chas.	H.	31
Hanser	Edward	A.	30
Hardenburgh	Alexander		28
Hardenburgh	Char. W. J.		14
Hardenburgh	John C.		28
Hardenburgh	Jon C.		13
Hardenburgh	R.	M.J.	34
Hardenburgh	Richard J.		19
Hardie	Charles		30
Harned	George		40
Harre	Augustus		44
Harrington	Stephen		25
Harrison	Marvin		39
Hartman	Benj.		31
Hartsough	Thomas		40
Harviland	Albert		40
Hathaway	Wm.	H.	40
Havens	Ansel	B.	24
Havens	Samuel	H.	36
Hawk	Christian		34
Hawley	David	S.	28
Hayes	Michael		40
Hazen	Jeremiah		33
Hector	Albert		32
Hector	Hiram		37
Hemingway	Henry H.		21
Hemingway	Henry H.		39
Hemmingway	Chauncy		40
Hemmingway	Orlando		40
Hendershot	Chas. W.		26
Hendrickson	Blake		23
Hendrickson	Elias		43
Hendrickson	John M.		20
Hendrickson	Jon. H.		43
Hendrickson	Richard C.		33
Hendrixson	Wm.		22
Hibbard	George		26
Hickey	John		44
Higgins	John		13
Higgins	John		25
Hilderbrant	Elihu		39
Hill	Ellas	B.	43
Hill	Fillmore		32
Hill	George		37
Hill	Granger		30
Hill	James		42
Hill	Matthew		23

56

Surname	First	Initial	Page
Hill	Wallace		39
Hill	Wallace		16
Hill	William		22
Hill	Wm.	H.	42
Hitchcock	William		25
Hitt	Franklin		22
Hitt	Ira	F.	31
Hitt	James	M.	23
Hitt	Lewis		31
Hoaglen	Aaron		32
Hodge	James	H.	17
Hodge	Leander	A.	38
Hofer	John		30
Hoffman	Aaron		44
Hogancamp	John	M.	20
Hollinshead	Daniel		39
Hollis	Charles	S.	15
Holly	John	C.	24
Holmes	William		26
Hood	George	W.	23
Horace	Russell		24
Horgin	Jefferson		26
Hornbeck	John		21
Hosa	John		20
Hosie	John	P.	33
Houghtaling	John		24
Houghtaling	Sands	R	24
Housten	Edmund		15
How	James	T.	40
Howard	Edward	C.	19
Howard	Edward	C.	13
Howard	George		28
Howard	John	M.	37
Hoxie	William	W.	16
Hoyt	Jonathan	M.	28
Hoyt	Lewis	N.	17
Hu-chen	Andrew		32
Huber	Nicholas		31
Huber	Ulrich		31
Huff	Lewis		30
Hull	Aaron	B.	33
Hulslander	William		40
Hunt	Abram	C.	17
Hunt	John		15
Huntington	Edward	H.	37
Hurd	John		40
Hurley	Elisha		40
Hutchins	Chester	D.	35
Ingric	Walter		44
Irons	George	H.	37
Jackson	Alexander		31
Jackson	Chas.		31
Jackson	Dan		19

Surname	First	Initial	Page
Jackson	John	H.	19
Jacob	Albert	L.	25
Jacobs	John	H.	19
Jacoby	Robert	E.	30
Jelliff	Isaac		43
Jelliff	Isaac		18
Johnson	Dennis		34
Johnson	Norman	C.	25
Jones	Benj.		23
Jones	Jonathan		23
Joselyn	John	W.	15
Joyner	Joseph		18
Jugger	Frank		39
Kanise	Louis		16
Kearney	Benjamin	W.	34
Keeler	Bailey	S.	15
Keeler	David	H.	15
Keen	Gilbert		16
Keesler	Augustus	H.	43
Keesler	Conrad		44
Keesler	Solomon		42
Keesler	Wallace		42
Kellam	A.	C.	34
Kellam	Peter		33
Kellem	Sandswirtte	D.	34
Kent	Charles		20
Kent	George	A.	18
Kent	Jacob		18
Kent	Rurr	S.	18
Kerr	Samuel		33
Kile	George	W.	38
Kimball	Herman		31
Kimball	James		34
Kinne	Dan	L.	20
Kizer	Albert		40
Knapp	John	L.	43
Knapp	John	L.	27
Knapp	Nelson		34
Knapp	William		33
Knickerbocker	Clay	E.	40
Kniffen	Benjamin		36
Kniffen	James	H.	28
Knox	Adna	L.	22
Krum	Herman	M.	15
Krum	Luther	S.	20
Krum	Peter	L.	34
Kyrk	Ephraim	E.	33
Laden	William	O.	43
Lair	James	D.	37
Lambert	Adam		34
Lambesson	James	E.	40
Lambesson	Wm.		40
Laning	Stephen		33

Surname	First	Initial	Page
Laraway	Abram		14
Laraway	Abrm.		15
Laraway	Henry		15
Laraway	Martimus		15
Laraway	Wilson		15
Lawrence	Gilbert		23
Lawrence	Peter	E.	21
Lawson	Benjamin		20
Layman	Alston		36
Layton	Chas.	B.	25
Layton	Chas.	B.	42
Lee	Amos		44
Leib	Theodore		30
Lent	Charles		42
Lent	Henry	J.	43
Lent	Joseph	A.	43
Lent	Nath'l	V.	17
Lent	Thomas	O.	42
Leonard	Levi		28
Leroy	Peter	H.	23
Leslie	James	E.	21
Lewis	Chas.	W.	37
Lewis	Edward	A.	32
Lewis	Joseph	P.	36
Lewis	Reuben	A.	21
Lewis	Samuel	A.	36
Lewis	William	B.	21
Lillie	Harrison		42
Lindsay	Chas.	W.	26
Linson	Lyan	S.	19
Litts	Thomas	H.	15
Lockwood	Daniel	C.	22
Logan	Charles		26
Lohman	Adam		17
Long	John		31
Longcoy	Harrison		24
Loomis	Amon		26
Lord	James		15
Lord	Joseph	H.	17
Lord	Samuel		15
Lorgan	James	D.	19
Loring	Jonathan	C.	18
Louesi	Marianna		35
Lounsbury	John	M.	17
Low	James		21
Low	Jonathan	W.	22
Luckey	William	V.	35
Luckley	T.	B.	34
Lybolt	Henry	C.	18
Lyon	George		20
Lyson	John		32
Mackey	Linns	S.	25
Mackney	Samuel		23

Surname	First	Initial	Page
Maffitt	Ferris		36
Mallon	Barney		24
Maltby	Marcus		31
Maltby	Marcus		23
Manett	George	V.	21
Mapledoram	James	C.	17
Maricle	William	P.	21
Marold	Paul		42
Marold	Robert		42
Martin	Gideon	W.	23
Marvin	John	B.	36
Mason	James	B.	17
Mason	John	H.	43
Masten	Abrm.		25
Masten	David	W.	27
Mathews	David		13
Matthews	James	H.	24
Matthews	Lorenzo		23
Maxwell	Edward		40
McCord	Andrew	J.	17
McDermott	James		41
McGovern	Patrick		27
McGusy	Matthew		42
McIntyre	John	L.	18
McKellip	Enos	C.	36
McLaughlin	Henry	C.	27
McLynn	James		38
McMillen	William		16
McPherson	Charles	J.	17
McPherson	Chas.	J.	13
McPhillemy	Robert		37
McRoe	William		39
McWhorter	John	T.	39
McWilliams	Chas.	S.	33
McWilliams	John		17
McWilliams	Wesley		24
Mead	Jacob		25
Mead	William	H.	17
Mearns	Samuel		24
Meddeuch	Abrm.		22
Meddler	Wm.	O.	22
Medler	Zachariah		27
Mericle	VanGosbeck		25
Meyers	John	Jr.	34
Middaugh	Denis	S.	17
Miller	David		23
Miller	George		32
Miller	George		30
Miller	Henry		30
Miller	John		30
Miller	Lewis	H.	42
Miller	Samuel	J.	15
Miller	Verdine	H.	34

Surname	First	Initial	Page
Milligan	William	G.	34
Mills	George	H.	30
Mills	Seth	B.	31
Misner	George	R.	32
Mitchell	Joseph		25
Mitchell	Wm.	H.	30
Mix	Henry		26
Mock	Philip		44
Moffat	William	S.	39
Morey	William	A.	40
Morgan	Chester	S.	24
Morgan	Isaac		21
Morgan	Patrick		38
Morgan	William	T.	14
Morgans	William	T.	33
Morgans	Wm.	F.	31
Morris	Goerge	J.	15
Morris	James	D.	18
Morris	John		42
Morrison	Edward		26
Morse	John	W.	36
Mosher	Philip		40
Muir	David		27
Murphy	Edward		26
Murray	William		32
Murry	Adolphus	E.	37
Murry	Andrew		36
Murry	George		31
Murry	Thomas		44
Myers	Adelbert		17
Myers	George		24
Myers	Moses	D., Jr.	15
Myers	William	D.	15
Myers	William	H.	15
Nash	David		39
Nation	Joseph	W.	28
Newman	Austin	D.	23
Newman	Thomas		15
Newman	William	H.	21
North	C.	Howell	43
North	C. Howell		25
Norton	Edward	J.	31
Norton	James		24
Norton	John		31
Norton	Will.	H.	25
Norton	Willis		31
Nugent	John		41
O'Brian	John		38
Odell	Jesse	H.	33
Oneil	Terrace		20
Ormsby	Floran	D.	26
Osborn	Peter	V.	16
Osborne	Robert		26

Surname	First	Initial	Page
Osterhout	Cornelius		42
Osterhout	Gideon		38
Osterhout	Wm.	H.	44
Oudet	C.	G. A.	17
Ousterhout	Geo.	W.	33
Overacker	Isaac		40
Palen	Peter	E.	42
Palen	Peter	E.	22
Palmanteer	Abrm.		31
Palmer	Asha	B.	18
Palmer	John	J.	21
Palmer	Rufus		19
Parker	Geo.	W.	30
Parliman	William	H.	37
Patmore	David	A.	22
Pattergill	Florel		40
Patterson	John		25
Patterson	John		19
Payne	John		40
Peas	Almond		39
Peck	John	P.	26
Pendell	Sidney	T.	31
Pendergrass	John		42
Penney	George	C.	16
Pentlar	John	C.	19
Pentlar	Will.		20
Perhamous	Emery		22
Perkey	Elijah	P.	23
Perrigo	Chas.	M.	40
Perry	George		42
Perry	Seneca	W.	19
Perry	Seneca	W.	13
Pierce	John	W.	28
Pierce	Joseph		15
Pinney	Edward	H.	30
Pinney	George	C.	36
Pinney	George	C.	31
Piper	Jacob	H.	25
Pollock	Robert		27
Porter	Henry	W.	37
Porter	Orson		36
Porter	Rufus	W.	37
Powell	Joseph		43
Powell	Russell		23
Poyer	Aaron		24
Pratt	John	M.	28
Pratt	Samuel		41
Presonins	Cornelius	B.	24
Price	Henry	R.	28
Price	James		17
Price	Solomon		25
Priestley	John		30
Pringle	John		25

Surname	First	Initial	Page
Punderbaugh	Theodore		40
Purvis	George	W.	16
Purvis	John	E.	17
Putler	Patrick		19
Quackenbush	Franklin		16
Quick	Cyrus	J.	30
Quick	DeWitt		26
Quick	John	J.	44
Quick	Joshua		43
Race	Austin	A.	27
Race	Mortimer		27
Ralston	George		18
Rambour	August		17
Rambour	August		13
Randolph	Charles		24
Ratcliff	Wm.	B.	13
Ray	Edward		20
Reed	Samuel		27
Reese	Chas.	G.	38
Reynolds	Benj.		34
Reynolds	Hezekiah	J.	27
Reynolds	Hiram	T.	34
Reynolds	John	W.	32
Reynolds	Nelson	T.	22
Reynolds	Sam'l	M.	26
Reynolds	Wm.	H.	34
Richard	John		28
Richard	Louis	P.	16
Rizir	Jacob		39
Robbins	David	B.	25
Robbinson	David		24
Roberts	John	W.	26
Roberts	Francis	W.	25
Robertson	Clark	J.	32
Robertson	Levi		16
Robinson	Langton		39
Robinson	William		33
Robison	Philip	S.	18
Rockafellow	Ches.	B.	34
Roosa	Francis	M.	23
Roosa	John	E.	23
Roosa	William	M.	36
Roover	John		29
Rose	Austin	J.	19
Rose	Caleb	G.	31
Rose	Garrett		36
Rose	George	W.	34
Rose	Gustavus		36
Rose	Gustavus		19
Rose	Hiram	E.	36
Rose	James	Jr.	30
Rose	Seth	B.	38
Rose	William	E.	34

Surname	First	Initial	Page
Rose	William	M.	30
Ross	John	G.	43
Row	Samuel	A.	22
Rowe	Orrin	D.	23
Rumsey	Cyrus		18
Rumsey	George		32
Rumsey	John	J.	18
Ryan	Michael		32
Ryder	Jacob	T.	34
Ryder	William		39
Sackett	James		43
Sanab	Alfred		30
Sarine	Ira		28
Sarine	Jacob		29
Saunders	John	B.	43
Schoonmaker	Elijah		27
Schoonmaker	Moses	H.	23
Schoonmaker	Moses		23
Schryver	Chas.	H.	24
Scott	Adam		35
Scott	George	W.	27
Scutt	Socrates		40
Seaman	James	H.	34
Seaman	Peter		39
Searle	Jeremiah		13
Secor	Lorenzo		18
Seeley	James	L.	34
Seeley	Sanford	L.	34
Shafer	Jacob	E.	37
Shave	John	W.	39
Shaw	Henry		40
Shaw	Henry		25
Shaw	Levi		27
Shaw	Thomas	J.	29
Shaw	William		41
Sheeley	Calvin		38
Sheeley	Tobias	C.	23
Sheeley	Tobias		17
Sheely	David	J.	17
Sherwood	John		40
Sherwood	Morgan		41
Sherwood	Roswell	F.	38
Sherwood	Wm.	P.	41
Shields	Chas.	J.	34
Short	Lewis	H.	31
Shultis	Wm.	H.	21
Siebecker	Lewis		30
Simpson	Allen		33
Simpson	Andrew	J.	28
Simpson	Chas.	H.	23
Sinsabaugh	Jacob	H.	27
Sisson	Will.	D.	19
Skillmore	James	M.	40

Surname	First	Initial	Page
Skinner	Benj.	A.	29
Skinner	Lewis		27
Skinner	Samuel	W.	28
Skinner	Samuel	L.	28
Skinner	Theodore		27
Skinner	Weston	D.	43
Slater	Albert	H.	18
Slater	Stephen		38
Slocum	Truxton		24
Smith	Arthur	W.	16
Smith	Charles	A.	28
Smith	Charles	A.	16
Smith	Edward	P.	31
Smith	George	H.	31
Smith	George		16
Smith	James		18
Smith	Lawrence		41
Smith	Orrin	B.	17
Smith	Thomas		39
Smith	William	H.	44
Smith	William	J.	38
Smith	William	C.	31
Smith	William		17
Smith	Willliam		18
Smth	Chas.	A.	27
Snow	Will.	G.	25
Snyder	Henry	J.	40
Spencer	Elijah		28
Sprague	DeWitt	C.	22
Sprague	Lafayette		37
St. John	Wm.	J.	29
Stahl	John		43
Stanton	Charles	C.	19
Stanton	John	S.	19
Stanton	Lewis	N.	25
Stanton	Lewis	N.	43
Starr	Bielby	P.	39
Starr	Sanford	M.	22
Stephens	Lewis		24
Stewart	James	H.	24
Stewart	James	W.	21
Stewart	Levi		33
Stickles	Andrew	J.	37
Stoddard	William		36
Stratton	Cyrus	J.	23
Stratton	George	W.	16
Stuart	Wm	H.	13
Sturdevant	George		14
Sturdevant	George		17
Sturdevant	LeGrand		25
Sturdevent	Franklin		33
Sutter	Henry		20
Sutton	Adolphus		42

Surname	First	Initial	Page
Sutton	John	S.	39
Swain	William	H.	41
Swalm	Lewis		42
Swarthout	Alex.	E.	23
Swarthout	George	M.	30
Sweet	John	D.	28
Taft	Joseph	B.	13
Taggett	Henry	F.	16
Tanner	Garrett		39
Tarket	DeWitt	C.	28
Tarket	Levi	W.	27
Taylor	James	M.	23
Taylor	William	J.	22
Teller	Horace	D.	35
Terry	Seth	A.	16
Terwilliger	Aaron		27
Terwilliger	Benj.		23
Terwilliger	Chas.	O.	40
Terwilliger	Sevryn	M.	23
Thomas	Nathan	M.	33
Thompson	Andrew	J.	31
Thompson	Jas.	H.	29
Thompson	John		16
Tice	Horton		27
Tice	Paul	P.	33
Tillotson	Robert	L.	17
Tillson	Jesse		28
Todd	John		34
Tomlinson	Robt.		41
Tompkins	Daniel	D.	28
Tompkins	Jehial	C.	29
Tompkins	Leonard		33
Tompkins	Nicholas		41
Tracy	George		43
Travis	Chas.	W.	37
Travis	George	W.	16
Travis	Orrin		19
Travisse	William		29
Tremper	John		31
Tripp	Peter	C.	21
Troomey	Timothy		24
Truce	George		24
Tucker	William		19
Turner	Henry		34
Turner	Nathaniel		35
Tuttle	Isaac	F.	44
Tyler	Lamando		44
Tyler	William		42
Tyler	William		34
Tyrell	William		22
Upham	George	W.	21
Urben	Henry		43
Van Valkenburgh	Osa		24

Surname	First	Initial	Page
Van Wagner	George	W.	21
Van Wert	Geo.	W.	44
VanLuven	Joachin	H.	29
VanLuven	John		27
VanOrden	Moses		24
VanOrden	Peter		17
VanOrder	George		24
VanOrman	Geo.	B.	24
VanSiclen	Theodore	C.	17
VanTassall	Philip		31
Vantran	John		19
Vantrum	James		43
VanWagnon	Herman		42
Verwimp	John		33
VonArr	Herman		30
VonArx	Rudolph		31
Vredenburgh	Henry	H.	22
Vredenburgh	Henry	J.	22
Vredenburgh	Jacob	C.	21
Waddell	Niel	H.	18
Wade	Jacob	S.	27
Wager	Enos		38
Wagner	David	H.	20
Wagner	Frank		17
Wait	Andrew		40
Wait	Henry	B.	39
Wait	James		41
Wales	John		16
Walker	James		31
Walker	John	Jacob	35
Wallestine	Lewis		43
Wamsley	John		23
Ward	Al.		40
Ward	Harry		36
Ward	Joseph		37
Warling	Stephen		34
Warmsley	Warner		34
Warner	Hughes		34
Warring	Graham		37
Warring	Hiram	B.	19
Warring	John	W.	20
Wasim	David	A.	19
Wasim	David	A.	15
Waterbury	Peter	L.	28
Watkins	Hezekiah		16
Watkins	Hezekiah		13
Watson	John	C.	40
Watson	Martin		20
Watts	George	B.	18
Watts	John	C.	18
Watts	Thomas		35
Watts	Thomas		34
Weber	Sohn		19

Surname	First	Initial	Page
Welsh	James		41
Wever	Philip	A.	24
Wheeler	John	H.	43
Wheeler	Lewis	S.	18
Wheeler	Wallace	W.	13
Whipple	Chas.	C.	37
Whiston	David	W.	17
White	Abrm.		23
White	Joe		20
White	Nelson	S.	24
Whitley	George	W.	20
Whitmarsh	Chauncy		31
Whitmarsh	Sanford		38
Whitmore	Andrew	J.	29
Whittaker	Henry		22
Wickham	George		39
Wicks	Charles		21
Willcox	Lyman		41
Williams	Burroughs		43
Williams	Henry	H.	30
Williams	Mark	L.	32
Wilson	Andrew	S.	22
Wilson	Edward	B.	40
Wilson	James	B.	22
Wingart	John		31
Winner	Solomon		37
Winslow	Joseph		31
Wood	Hezekiah		16
Wood	Jerome		43
Wood	Samuel		24
Woodmancy	George		39
Woodruff	Wesley	J.	42
Woodward	Archibald		37
Wormouth	Alfred		31
Wormouth	Isaac		32
Wormouth	Stephen		31
Wright	Charles		16
Wright	George	W.	41
Wright	George	R.	15
Wright	Joseph		18
Yeomans	Benj.	M.	20
Yeomans	William	H.	18
York(s)	Herman		16
Yorks	Nicholas		20
Young	Eber	C.	37
Young	George		16
Young	Gilbert	I.	17
Young	Jeriah		33
Young	Jirah	J.	37
Young	Matthew		29
Young	Moses		15
Young	Robert		38
Yowkee	Henry		30

<u>NOTES</u>

NOTES

NOTES

Made in the USA
Las Vegas, NV
13 February 2024

85754100R00049